"The comparison trap ⌐ ₒ ᵥᵢᵥᵢₒᵤₛ cycle for women. *Measuring Up* helps break this cycle and is a must-read for every woman, mom, business owner, and social media user!"
—**Rachel Pedersen**, CEO at The Viral Touch, Social Media United

"Comparison depletes our joy, drains our resources, and debilitates our prospects, so why do we so often find ourselves imprisoned by its insidious power? In *Measuring Up* Renee Vidor tackles this subject and offers hope to all who want to escape its trap. Through her vulnerable storytelling and wise advice, Renee will gracefully help you back onto a path of confidence."
—**Skip Prichard**, CEO of OCLC, Inc. & WSJ Bestselling Author of *The Book of Mistakes: 9 Secrets to Creating a Successful Future*

"Renee Vidor nailed it! We have always been a people who have compared ourselves to others but when social media hit the scene, our measuring sticks just got longer. Before our first cup of coffee, most of us have scrolled through our social feeds and compared ourselves in one way or another. In *Measuring Up*, one will find hope and confidence- perhaps for the very first time. I'm grateful to be able to offer such a resource to my community."
—**Shari Braendel**, Founder of Fashion Meets Faith and Author of *Help Me, Jesus, I have nothing to wear!*

"Comparison is a thief. It can rob you of so many things. Many of us have spent the greater portion of our lives dismissing our joy, limiting our potential, and disregarding our purpose based on the idea of not measuring up.

Thank you, Renee, for your transparency in this amazing book. *Measuring up* is a call to action for you to reclaim your narrative and move toward your destiny."
—**Noni Banks**, founder and CEO of
The Diva Movement Inc.

"With a mission to help inspire girls to fearlessly pursue their dreams with passion and confidence, I see firsthand how comparison gets in the way. *Measuring Up* provides an innovative solution to reclaiming control so that we can be the unstoppable women we were created to be."
—**Sandra Brogdon**, founder and Creative
Director of *Role Model Magazine*

"Comparison is a human condition. As a spouse, parent, and CEO, the temptation to look around and feel like I'm not quite measuring up is real. Renee Vidor is right: Comparison will always attempt to steer our lives, but we get to choose what we measure ourselves against. Eternity is at stake. Everyone needs the simple, life-altering process shared in this book so they can truly win in the game of life."
—**Kary Oberbrunner**, author of *Your Secret Name*
and *Day Job to Dream Job*

"Don't believe the lie that having more, looking better, or winning a contest equates to happiness. It doesn't. *Measuring Up* is a much-needed message. Renee's honesty and experience make this book relatable to all women as she shows us exactly how to claim control over comparison in our lives so we can confidently share our message with the world!"
—**Lisa Moser**, former *Miss Ohio USA*, *Mrs. International*, and author of *Miss Conception*

"Renee takes a raw, yet compassionate look at comparison and offers a fascinating, comprehensive, and easy to read process that resonates at the soul level. Teens, stay-at-home parents, and corporate executives will all be inspired to navigate life's journey with greater purpose and clarity. I dream of a world in which each child of God can shed the confusion of comparison and claim their God-given destiny without fear or shame. This book will be an important step in that journey."
— **Lisa Rae Morris**, author of *Wifeology,*
A Field Guide to the Wife In Her Natural Habitat;
and *The Time Tree Chronicles* series

Comparison can be ugly and messy, but it doesn't have to be. I wish I had this book before I allowed comparison to ruin my business. *Measuring Up* taught me the right tools and mindset to take control instead of giving comparison the wheel. If you're done with always trying to measure up to the world and ready to start being your authentic self, this book is a must read!
— **Jeff Elder**, founder of *Do Business God's Way*

As a working single parent, I needed this book as I navigated through divorce, health, career, and parenting issues. Renee lovingly and thoughtfully steers us toward a healthier present to create a more fulfilled future. *Measuring Up* offers strategies we may all put into practice immediately!
— **Wendy Hamby**, parent and educator

Though I often experience a strange, uneasy feeling, it wasn't until reading *Measuring Up* that I learned why: Comparison! The answers for controlling comparison and focusing on your true destination are within this book. Goodbye anxiety—hello confidence!
— **Noriko Kitamura**, former *Miss Universe Japan* top 10 finalist

MEASURING
UP

HOW TO WIN IN A WORLD
OF COMPARISON

MEASURING UP

HOW TO WIN IN A WORLD OF COMPARISON

RENEE VIDOR

AUTHOR
ACADEMY

Identifiers:

LCCN: 2019933636
Softcover: 978-1-64085-590-8
Hardcover: 978-1-64085-591-5
E-book: 978-1-64085-592-2

Available in paperback, hardback, e-book, and audiobook

Book design by Jetlaunch.

For my sweet daughter, Ariela, who continually inspires me to become the woman I was created to be. My prayer for you is that you'll always know *who* you are, and *Whose* you are.

And for every woman struggling to measure up— may you soon be who you're created to be so you can do what you're designed to do.

CONTENTS

FOREWORD

It is my delight to honor Renee Vidor as you hold this book in your hands.

From the moment I met Renee, I knew there was something special about her. She cares about people—really cares. Over the years, Renee and I have been involved in a women's Bible study together and have enjoyed an international cooking class made up of women from several different countries. Many of these lovely ladies were invited by Renee. I've often joked about who she has "picked up" at the gym or grocery store because she so easily befriends people around her. She sees people. She listens. Then she invites and includes them. I've watched her lead, but also love behind the scenes when she thought no one was looking. Renee is a "there you are" kind of person rather than a "here I am" sort of gal.

Through Renee's journey with comparison, you will find glimpses of your own story. Comparison can be a tool that helps us grow and love others well, or it can be a destructive force that keeps us from living our best lives. Renee's stories and illustrations will inspire you to be cautious when looking sideways and learn to focus on the path laid out for you. As we discover our unique identity, we can indeed win in the world of comparison.

The truths in this book are invaluable, and I'm also thrilled you will get to know my sweet friend in these pages. Enjoy!

Melissa Spoelstra
Women's conference speaker;
award-winning author of
Total Family Makeover and *Jeremiah*

A NOTE TO THE READER

Hello fellow traveler! I'm so glad that our paths have crossed in this journey of life. My name is Renee and I want you to know how important you are to me. You may be a CEO, entrepreneur, bartender, stay-at-home-mom, or unemployed. Maybe you have a PhD, a GED, or a fourth-grade education. I don't care if you're a homebody or a Hollywood celebrity, are married, divorced, or single, have kids, want kids, or think kids are gross. *You are important and valuable.*

We all have different stories, experiences, and destinations. As much as our world tells us that our journeys are vertical ladders taking us a rung higher or lower than others, they're actually linear. We live our lives in parallel lines and we have so much to learn from one another.

One thing that connects us on this journey is the natural tendency to compare and to feel judged—including judging ourselves. I know you've dealt with Comparison at some point along your journey and have thought, "I'll never measure up," or, "I can never win!"

Me too, sister. Whether comparing ourselves to individuals, expectations or societal norms, it's easy to lose control and let Comparison navigate our journey—and it hurts. I can see you nodding your head, and I wish I could reach through these pages and give you a big hug. This topic weighs heavy on my heart because I allowed Comparison to dictate my life and enslave me for far too long. Along this journey, I learned a three-step process that helped me take control over Comparison, and I'm so excited to share it with you! This process, called the WIN Method, has helped me to experience the freedom to be who I'm created to be—I believe it can be the vehicle toward your freedom, too.

Throughout this book, I'll use the metaphor of driving a car. Imagine life's journey as driving a vehicle down the highway toward your destination—whatever that may be. Keep this image in mind as you encounter many of the analogies, including Comparison being an entity that tries to steal your wheel and take control of your journey (this is why you'll see *Comparison* capitalized like a proper noun).

To the readers who may be less inclined to resonate with the word "comparison"—you're dealing with the same phenomenon; perhaps you would call it *competition*. The situations and semantics vary on account of personal differences—and even gender—but Comparison *is* costing you. Though I primarily address the ladies throughout these pages, men will benefit, too. Men, you'll be able to better understand and help your female counterparts as you learn what they're going through; but I also guarantee you'll walk away with helpful nuggets to apply to your life.

I don't claim to have it all together. Simply writing this book forced me to test the WIN Method. Comparison often challenged me with thoughts such as, *You're a terrible writer* or *you're an imposter; you're no expert,* and *you have no business writing this book.* Though many authors complete their book proposal within two weeks, months had passed since I had agreed to write *Measuring Up,* and my proposal was still incomplete. *Seriously, what is my problem? I stink at this!*

As I sat working on the proposal and mentally beating myself up, a Facebook post appeared on my screen. The woman's words instantly grabbed my attention.

"The beauty of what is precious to me . . . doesn't seem to measure up to others . . . Comparison has kept me quiet for many years. . . ."

It was as if she wrote that for me!

The woman further shared how Comparison kept her from moving forward with her dreams because seeing other people's big goals and dreams made her dreams seem little and insignificant. Her words were a mirror to my soul reflecting back how I was giving Comparison the wheel to my writing journey.

I looked at influencers with bigger platforms successfully tackling problems which appeared to be more significant than the message I felt led to convey. This woman's post reminded me of the importance of my message. Those standing on their successful platforms did so because they focused on *their* destination, not someone else's.

It was time to turn my side-glancing into my fuel instead of my brake. By applying the same WIN Method that I'll soon teach you—Weighing my costs, Innovating my identity and Navigating my journey—I quickly regained control of Comparison and completed the proposal.

The same applies for you. You can buy this book—even read it to the end—but until you repeatedly apply the principles outlined within it to your personal life journey, Comparison will continue to steal your wheel.

Commit to being honest with yourself as you read and operate in a no-shame zone. You won't find any judgment from me, so don't judge or condemn yourself, either. Everyone experiences feelings of inadequacy from time to time. I've divulged some of my own vulnerable emotions, as well as stories from other women (most names have been changed to protect privacy). We are all growing and learning.

You are about to discover what Comparison is, what it's costing you, how to obtain the best benchmark to measure up to, and ultimately, how to gain control. You'll soon have the tools necessary to travel life in the freedom and joy of being who you're created to be and doing what you're designed to do.

It's time to buckle up and start your engine! Let's embark on this road trip together and learn how we can measure up and win in this world of Comparison!

Your Friend on the Journey,
Renee

PART ONE
WEIGH YOUR COST

CHAPTER ONE

The World of Comparison: What's Comparison have to do with me?

> **Comparison** (n)
> The act or instance of comparing.

Imagine a life where you could choose your clothing each morning based on comfort and your makeup and hair routines were optional instead of the unspoken rule. Picture a place where a number on the scale didn't determine how worthy you felt. Think about feeling safe and satisfied living within your financial means because a house, car, and possessions didn't define you. Contemplate a world where your career and life decisions were based on your passions and interests versus accolades, titles, and the alphabet soup following your name.

Envision walking into a new situation—a playgroup, a church, a social event, or a client meeting—without a racing heart, dripping palms, and self-deprecating thoughts. No more thoughts of *will I fit in?* to keep you from being present in your current situation.

As you read through this book, we'll discuss how much control you *think* you have over Comparison in your life and how to determine what level of control you *really* have. Then, we'll work together to get you to the place you want to be . . . completely in charge of Comparison.

Just imagine how free you will feel when you have thrown away the mental checklists of the ways you need to change in order to measure up. How would you feel if you could be *you?*

I asked myself that question many years ago. I would be free to be who I was created to be and to do what I'm designed to do—without any self-judgment or judgment from others. I yearned for this freedom.

Something was making me feel shackled. Stifled. *Not enough.* This *something* needed to be eliminated—or so I thought.

Then, I learned its name: *Comparison.*

Comparison was the obstacle between me and the wonderful world I imagined. Comparison told me I wasn't good enough, I shouldn't do *this*, I ought to do *that*. It told me I'd never measure up if I didn't comply.

I was sick of being its slave; I longed to be free from its control over my life.

This longing was a catalyst to eliminate Comparison from my life. I put forth my best efforts to stop comparing. I read books, studied research articles, and put my psychology schooling back to work. Most of the literature and articles were nothing more than a bunch of rhetoric around the idea of how bad it was to compare, and the advice was *don't do it.* That's not helpful. It's like telling someone who's obese to lose weight! If only it were that easy.

When I googled the phrase *how to stop comparing yourself to others,* over 43 million results populated for me. A few were:

> "Be a Unique Flower – How to Stop Comparing Yourself to Others"
> "How to Stop Comparing Yourself to Others, According to Experts"
> "Why You Compare Yourself to Other People (And How to Stop)"

With so many articles—many from well-known and reputable sources—you'd think we'd have the comparison conundrum figured out by now. No matter how many books I consumed, self-affirmations I recited, or people I pictured in third world countries who have it worse than I do, the Comparison struggle remained real, and I still didn't measure up.

There is a reason why we can't stop comparing. It's not for lack of effort. It's not because only a small percentage of the population have arrived and the rest of us never will. It's not because we don't want it badly enough or haven't tried the right trick.

It's because it's impossible.

As long as we are on this earth, Comparison will be a part of our lives. *Does this mean I'm doomed to feel like a loser who can never measure up in the game of life?*

Refusing to give up hope, I pressed on to find a better answer. After investing time and money in counseling and putting heartfelt effort into vulnerability and humility, I discovered that freedom is indeed possible. However, it looks vastly different than I once thought.

Comparison actually isn't entirely bad! Without Comparison, we'd live in a world lacking innovation and progress; there would be minimal motivation to do better or improve. We would accept everything as is without a question.

Instead of focusing on eliminating Comparison, we need to coexist with it and use it to our advantage. But first, we must stop giving it the keys to our life—we need to take control.

———⟊⟊⟊———

Things are not always as they appear. Meet Jill—successful business owner and entrepreneur. I looked up to Jill and enjoyed getting to know her. One evening after a networking event, Jill caught me off guard when she—intending it as a compliment—basically told me she was jealous of my life. In the interests of full transparency, I felt a twinge of flattery; but, how could *my* life be mistaken for a smooth Sunday cruise when I was constantly comparing myself to other women?

Apparently, from her window, I had it all together. Driving in the next lane, she saw me as a confident, successful business owner with a great husband in the front seat, two healthy, smart, happy kids in the back and a nice car driving on a freshly-paved lane.

The feeling of flattery quickly morphed into sadness. This woman didn't clearly see reality; Comparison controlled her life and showed her a false interpretation.

Nothing is ever what it seems. Sure, there was some truth to Jill's view—I have a great husband and wonderful children—but she was oblivious to my dings and dents and the bumpy journey I'd traveled. By staring out the window into my lane, she was missing the amazing scenery along the route to her destination.

I've been there many times. I've let Comparison sit in the driver's seat and sat staring out of my passenger seat window at other people's lives. We can never enjoy our journey when focusing on someone else's. After talking with many women who've been open and vulnerable, I've learned that many of us have allowed ourselves to

> We can never enjoy our journey when focusing on someone else's.

be victims of Comparison. You are *not* a victim! You are not alone in this struggle, but only you can choose to keep the keys to your life rather than handing them over to Comparison.

One such woman who has inspired me on this road to understanding is Cherie. When interviewing Cherie for her story, she shared a few pictures with me that help to remind her of where she's been. The first one revealed an attractive trim figure adorned in a sapphire blue bikini. She had long blond hair and a bright smile—she was stunning! I'd have never guessed by her outward appearance Cherie struggled with Comparison.

The picture was taken on the beach in Aruba, where Cherie and her husband had gotten away for a last-minute all-inclusive vacation. I listened to her share her story, envisioning the warm salty breeze, the peaceful white beaches, and no parental responsibilities. Who wouldn't want to trade places with this happily married couple sneaking away on a romantic getaway?

Or so I thought. . . .

The next picture showed Chad, her tall, dark, and handsome husband, holding her close as they stood on a beach with a rosy sunset background.

"You two look like you stepped off the cover of a romance novel!" I said.

Cherie chuckled. "A waiter did mistake us for honeymooners. I guess we put on a good front," she sighed, "however, I was longing to swap lives with any other couple there."

Cherie and Chad's marriage was running on fumes as they had recently experienced a major relational collision.

Three weeks prior to these pictures, Cherie had caught Chad having an affair. Though he chose to end the extramarital relationship when confronted, the damage done was severe. There was no room for romance as they attempted to figure out how to do life together again in the same lane. They were attempting to salvage the marriage and preserve the family their young daughter needed.

The affair left Cherie feeling like a failure. She felt ugly, unloved, and unwanted and longed to measure up to who she thought her husband wanted, but she didn't know how. Comparison hijacked her thought life and took her down Crazy Lane.

"The vacation was tough on me—everywhere I looked there were pretty women I knew Chad would be attracted to," Cherie confessed. "I became preoccupied with judging every female—analyzing them through the perception of what I thought my husband would want. I was subconsciously asking myself, *Do I look as good as her? Would he pick me over that girl?* I literally felt hostile toward women who intimidated me. I was a hot mess!"

When I asked Cherie to tell me about the mistress who had occupied Chad's affection, she showed me a private note she found written by Chad during his affair. There were two columns: Cherie's name was at the top of one and on the other was written his girlfriend's name, Tina. Underneath each name, he listed out the pros and cons for each woman—a Comparison list. He listed Cherie as *loyal* and *a good mom*. Tina was *fun*, made him *feel special* and was a *great companion*. I can only imagine how gut-wrenching it was for Cherie when she read this for the first time.

"I never met Tina in person," she said, "but I know more than enough to know she's nothing I logically would want to be.

"She was a porn actress-turned-stripper with STDs, bad intentions, and fake boobs that would make Dolly Parton gasp. But I was hurt. And jealous. I gave Comparison full access to my mind and became obsessed with learning about Tina, which turned into a longing to become her. I wanted to measure up to whatever it was my husband was looking for that I wasn't providing."

Weighing the cost of giving control to Comparison, Cherie realized it was causing internal mental anguish and costing her emotional energy. It also resulted in relational tension with other women and, of course, her husband. She was losing time—spending countless hours searching for ways to become what she perceived her husband wanted. This pursuit was stealing productivity from her job and time from her employer. In her attempt to be sexier in the way she thought her husband wanted, the shopping sprees for expensive outfits and lingerie cost her financially. She even consulted for a radical breast augmentation, but refrained from surgery at the last minute.

No one from the outside looking in would see how much Cherie was struggling and the affects that Comparison were having on her. She was a beautiful, well-liked, successful, and well-respected woman—but when she weighed what it was costing her, she knew she needed to take back control from Comparison.

Cherie eventually sought out help so she could win her battle with Comparison. She learned who she was created to be and how to measure up to her Innovated Identity instead of the fake identity she was trying to create. Only then was she able to begin navigating her journey confidently toward her destination instead of giving Comparison permission to drive her toward despair. We'll learn the process she used to accomplish this in the following chapters.

Pointing at the first picture of her on the beach, Cherie explained, "I didn't know who I was at that time, so I was trying to be someone else. In hindsight, it was a bad situation no matter what, but I would've avoided so much extra pain if I hadn't gotten caught up in Comparison. The good news is, now I know who I am, and I love her! I am enough! It's so freeing to measure up and know that I'm able to be who I'm created to be."

Cherie's story is one of many that inspire me to share this message of hope. Anyone—no matter where they've driven or where they're currently parked—can choose to regain control of Comparison in their life and win. Yes, you too!

Cherie's story isn't every woman's story, but we've all had some encounter with Comparison and lost control.

Your struggle with Comparison may not center on physical appearance or measuring up as a wife. Perhaps you wrestle with comparing the number of clients you have to your competitors. It could be your salary, the achievements you've earned, the quality of your relationships, or the total followers and likes you have on social media. Regardless of how Comparison controls your life, *you are not alone.* Our experiences, wounds, insecurities, and unmet desires shape our interaction with Comparison. Nevertheless, we are all affected by it.

Comparison isn't only a modern-day problem; it's always been an issue. As far back as antiquity, we see evidence of humans' power struggle with Comparison. Take, for instance, the story of Creation. God created the universe and the first human being. Realizing that this man, Adam, needed a companion and helper, He formed a creature similar to Adam and named her Eve.

Then God was pleased with His Creation (and every woman who's ever felt like they don't measure up to their male counterparts can be encouraged).

Adam and Eve lived together in the garden of paradise where God said they could eat from any tree, except for *The Tree of the Knowledge of Good and Evil*—that one would cause them to die. Life was perfect until a sly serpent slithered into the picture with an agenda to destroy God's Creation. The snake knew he could succeed if the humans were to eat from the unauthorized tree. Any idea how he gained access to Eve's mind, conning her into eating the forbidden fruit?

You guessed it—Comparison.

A master of manipulation, the serpent asked Eve, "Did God *really* say you can't eat from any tree in the garden?"

"Not exactly," she replied, "He said we could eat from all but one, or we'll die."

"Ha!" The serpent hissed, "You won't die! He knows your eyes will be opened when you eat it, and you'll be just like God, knowing both good and evil." Then, she ate the forbidden fruit and shared it with Adam.

Hmm . . . she would be *like God.* That's Comparison speaking.

My friend, don't miss this key factor: When Eve compared herself to God, she was no longer content with who she was created to be—she wanted to be more like Him instead.

Eve chose to give Comparison the wheel, and the costs of her decision added up quickly. Here are a few that I noticed when reading further into the story:

Shame.

Eating the fruit caused their eyes to be opened to their nakedness, causing them to feel shame for the first time.

Fear.

Adam hid when God called out to him because he was afraid. He had never experienced fear previously.

Blame. Defensiveness. Rationalization.

When God asked Adam if he had eaten from the forbidden tree, Adam got defensive and blamed it on his wife, who rationalized that the serpent had deceived her.

Relational Problems.

A curse entered the world, causing physical and emotional pain.

Hard Work.

The ground was cursed, causing thorns and weeds to emerge. Food had always been provided, but now they had to work for it through planting and harvesting.

Death.

The first death took place when an animal was killed to provide clothes to cover Adam and Eve and alleviate their shame.

The ultimate cost was the separation that replaced the unity humanity once had with God.

Comparison having control affects more than the person who initially hands over the wheel. Eve's decision to allow Comparison to be the driving force in her mind cost her—and the rest of humanity—more than she could have imagined.

Some may believe Comparison was the catalyst for the fall of humankind, while others feel it is merely an ancient moral story. Either way, scholars agree the account was written around 3,000 years ago, proving Comparison to be an ongoing struggle in the minds of humans. Yes, it's in our human nature—but it's our choice to claim control or not.

Our modern world immerses us in Comparison. Technology provides endless opportunities to compare ourselves to others with our 24/7 uninterrupted view of the outside world. Our smartphones ding with social media notifications and force-feed us images of all life has to offer—and it's not what we are experiencing currently. In our peripheral vision, we see celebrities, coworkers, friends, family members—sometimes even our past selves—and we feel like we don't measure up to what we see.

Without any proof or factual information, we buy into Comparison-controlled thinking and fail to verify its legitimacy. Instead, we make Comparison the driver in our life, and we climb into the backseat, pouting about how lousy our life is compared to everyone else's.

When Comparison is in charge, it causes emotional pain, tension, and adverse side effects in many ways. Unrefined and improperly interpreted comparisons shape political beliefs, business interactions, relationships, and even major personal decisions. It's no wonder our world is in the state it is in. It can feel hopeless, but don't be fooled—that's what Comparison wants you to experience! There is a way to win, and it starts with you.

Let's begin by learning more about Comparison and the importance of coexisting with it.

Is Comparison All Bad?

Comparison is multi-faceted. As much as we blame Comparison for many of our problems, in and of itself, it isn't an evil villain. It can actually be beneficial when used properly. It's part of our human makeup and isn't going away, so we might as well learn how to coexist and capitalize on its positive potential. You may be asking, *How can it help me to compare?*

Here are four examples of benefits that Comparison can offer:

1. *Comparing can help us obtain a more accurate self-evaluation.*

   When we compare ourselves to others, we get a benchmark of ourselves personally and our situation. Psychologists call this "Social Comparison Theory."[1]

   Basically, we look around at everyone else and rank ourselves to find the answer to the question, "How am I doing?" Comparison helps us recognize if we need improvement in certain areas, or if we're doing fine.

2. *Comparing ourselves to others helps us find comfort.*

   Think of a time when you were entering into a new situation where everyone else was established—perhaps as a student going to a new school, a business professional attending an unfamiliar meeting, or a mom taking her child to a new playgroup. Can you recall your feelings and actions?

   As a student, looking around assessing the classroom, you hoped for an open seat next to students who appeared to be in your comfort zone. Perhaps you noticed similarities to yourself. For instance, attentive, studious individuals typically don't choose to sit with the apathetic students snoring in the back row. Similarly, as a business professional—depending on your level of confidence—you may have scanned the room and thought, "I don't want to sit next to the lady who has it all together with perfect hair and expensive suit." You chose a seat next to someone less intimidating.

And moms, let's be honest. We all know that perfect mother you stay far away from during library story time—the one with the flat-ironed hair and flawless makeup, in a designer outfit with perfect kids sitting quietly. Between your kids bickering and crying, you were lucky to get out the door in matching clothes, no makeup, and your hair in a messy bun. The kids' clothes, now that's another story! We feel much more comfortable finding other moms who appear to be similar to us.

3. *Comparison helps us make better decisions, quicker.*

Most people have dreams and goals they want to accomplish that require time, resources, and effort—all of which are limited—in order to bring thoughts and ideas to fruition. Comparison can be beneficial in helping us to identify and prioritize what will help us most.

As a new business owner, you can only afford to attend one conference this year. After identifying two industry leaders you want to learn from, you realize they are speaking at two different conferences. By comparing the speakers to decipher which one will help you most, the decision for which conference to attend is made easier.

4. *Comparing ourselves to our Innovated Identity helps us to become who we were created to be.*

While we haven't yet introduced the concept of the Innovated Identity (and will not dive into it fully until later), simply put: your *Innovated Identity* is the measuring stick you get after evaluating your current identity, removing what doesn't belong and adding in what does. It's the *you* who you're created to be and are continually becoming. When we measure ourselves to our Innovated Identity, we are able to bridge the gaps and become closer to who we were created to be.

A word of caution: while Comparison can help us find our order, our place, and our comfort zone, any benefits will quickly become detriments if you give Comparison control. Comparison may seem to offer beneficial solutions that may actually be neutral, or, could even result in potholes on our journey.

For instance, comparing may appear to help us cope with insecurity, when in fact, most of our insecurities originate from Comparison. I don't care if you're the most confident individual in the world; insecurity will lurk around your life at some point. If no one else existed on this planet to compare yourself with—no other thoughts, values, visuals, or ideas but your own—what would make you feel insecure?

Nothing.

But we do commune with others, and our insecurities can stem from as far back as childhood. They may arise from comparisons directed at us *(Be careful what you eat; you're not as skinny as other girls)*, ones we assign to ourselves *(I'm the only one in my department who hasn't earned "Top Salesperson" yet)*, or one we perceive others are making about us *(I feel like my friend thinks I'm not as fun to be with as our mutual friend)*.

No one wants to feel inadequate. Although Comparison is at the root of these insecurities, it also attempts to help you deal with them through coping mechanisms.

One coping mechanism is to identify someone whom you perceive to be worse off or inferior to you in the area of your insecurity and compare yourself to them. This method is called *Downward Comparing*.[2] Here are a few examples:

The gal struggling with her weight compares herself to a larger woman and thinks, "At least I'm not as big as she is."

The underachieving sales rep compares herself to a coworker hired at the same time, thinking "At least I was promoted faster than he was."

The friend assuming her friend's thoughts, thinks, "Even if I'm not as fun to be around, at least I can afford to go out more often than she can."

These downward comparisons can be benign and harmless, or conversely, when Comparison is given the wheel, they can become arrogant and vicious. Whether good or bad, they help us feel better about ourselves by numbing the pain of our self-doubt. We can utilize this type of Comparison to our benefit to help us to feel better about ourselves in the short term while we grow and heal from our insecurities; however, the potential pothole here is the tendency to give Comparison control, which can quickly lead to negative outcomes, like bullying or stagnation, furthering the Comparison cycle.

Another way Comparison can attempt to take over is when we look at people further down the road than we are. Sometimes we notice their superior qualities, successes, or skills and put ourselves down until we eventually excuse ourselves from our goals or dreams. We reason, *If I can't measure up to them, then why even try?* Comparing ourselves with those we perceive as better than us is known as an *Upward Comparison*.[3] You think you'll never perform a task as well as the person you're comparing yourself to, or maybe you'll never complete it at all. So, what's the point of putting forth all of that time and effort? Why even try?

While Upward Comparing can have a positive result when focusing on your desire to improve your current level of ability, it's a slippery slope toward a negative effect of self-sabotage and intentionally letting yourself off the hook.

"I've dreamt of acting, but I wasn't born with Halle Berry's talent. I didn't even get the main cast in my high school play, so why waste my time in the church drama group now? I'll never measure up."

"My boss asked me to facilitate the quarterly leadership meeting next month. Last time Tanya facilitated; she's a great speaker and did a fantastic job—I'd look dumb compared to her."

When we sabotage ourselves and knock down our self-image, we talk ourselves out of pursuing dreams and goals—even when the potential for success is well within reach. Comparison can disguise itself as a genuine reason for embracing victim mentality, or even laziness. Don't tell yourself the lie that you'll never be as good as others, giving Comparison permission to drive you down a detour to that will waste your life.

Who Compares?

Everyone is a Comparaholic—though there are different degrees. Social comparison affects all humans and even at an early age, Comparison affects our lives. Studies show that children have thicker skin than adults when comparing their performance to that of their peers. However, when gender enters the equation, it's a different story. One study looked at four- and five-year-old preschoolers who performed a timed task of tracing circles. When finished, they were told that a peer (either same-gender, opposite gender, or gender-unidentified) did better than they did. When told that a same-gender or gender-unidentified peer performed better, they did better when they repeated the task, and their self-evaluations increased the second time. When told that an opposite-gender peer performed better, they performed the task slower the second time.

What's alarming is that even when telling all children after the second task that they performed better than their peers, there was no positive increase in self-evaluations for those who were initially told that an opposite-gender peer performed better than they had. The fact that none of the children's self-evaluations were increased once having the knowledge of being outperformed by the opposite gender at one point indicates that being compared to a peer of the opposite gender— even once—can cause ongoing negative consequences regarding behavior and self-assessment.[4]

Comparison certainly doesn't stop at childhood. Ladies, we are professionals at giving the wheel to Comparison, aren't we? Take a moment and release the pretense that you don't compare or judge other women and set aside all the masks that you hide behind. When looking at other women, we compare our hair, skin, bodies, sex appeal, shoes, clothes, and how the clothing looks on us. If we see another gal wearing the same dress that we own, our mind churns out comparisons about whether she looks better (or worse) in it than we do.

And it doesn't stop at fashion and looks. We compare our relationships, popularity, loneliness, health, parenting methods, kids, and cooking abilities (or lack thereof). We compare status by whether we are a stay at home mom living in our yoga pants or whether we go to work in professional business attire each day—either way, we are often jealous and judge each other.

We compare ourselves to women who are older and younger; women with extravagant lifestyles and those who are economically less fortunate; women we know well and those whom we've never met. As absurd as it is, we even compare ourselves to the fake photoshopped women on billboards, computers, our phone and TV who were created for the sole intent of advertising to us and making us compare. No woman is immune to Comparison's tactics.

Sometimes we compare intentionally, while other times our minds do it automatically without the thought ever reaching our consciousness. We then determine whether or not we measure up in our world based on the objective information that we subconsciously process.

Comparison doesn't discriminate by gender; it's willing to sneak into any vehicle and seize the wheel if the owner allows it. It is vital to understand Comparison from each gender's viewpoint so we can all work together to be culture-changers and put Comparison in its place. It can look a little different when men give Comparison control, but we'll cover that later.

Though Comparison is here to stay and controls much of the world around us, you get to decide whether or not you'll allow it to hijack *your* life.

Your choice: settle for defeat and allow it to be an ongoing roadblock detouring you off course, or, learn how to take control and be victorious while using Comparison to benefit your life journey. Wouldn't you prefer to use it to your advantage to improve your relationships, increase your productivity, and potentially elevate your finances and assets?

I'm sure you're ready to jump into the process; I promise we'll get there! Before we can obtain control over Comparison, we need to know how it generally takes control and affects us.

Over the next four chapters, we're going to discuss the three main comparison roadblocks: Assets, Appearances, and Achievements. These categories are not meant to be rigid; instead, they're there to help us understand the behind-the-scenes thought processing that occurs when Comparison attempts to take over the driver's seat of our lives.

By taking a more in-depth look into each of these categorical roadblocks, you'll learn about what's going on when you compare and discover the areas in which you tend to stall out most often along your journey. You've got to know what makes you weak to stay strong.

Are you curious how much of a Comparaholic you are? You can take the free assessment at ComparisonBook. com/comparaholic. On a scale of 1 to 10, what level of control do you think you have over Comparison in your life right now?

(total control) 1 2 3 4 5 6 7 8 9 10 (no control)

CHAPTER TWO

Roadblock of Assets:
They have more than I do.

> **Asset** (n)
> A useful or valuable thing, person, or quality.
> Synonyms: benefit, advantage, resource

Ever run into Target for a single item you need? You make a beeline toward the beauty department to grab nail polish remover when fashionably dressed mannequins catch your eye sporting those trendy new boots you've seen your friends wearing. Finding your size, you plop a pair in your cart.

As you pass by the housewares department, a modern dinner set beckons from the end cap. Your boss and his wife are coming for dinner on Friday—what would they think of your old chipped and scratched plates? Of course, the dishes are a must-have.

Oh, look! That gadget everyone is talking about in your Facebook group—it cooks frozen chicken in five minutes! Wouldn't that make life wonderful?

Before you know it, your cart is overflowing with items that you never intended to buy. Talk about one expensive bottle of nail polish remover!

There's nothing wrong with having nice things. Stuff, in and of itself, usually isn't a problem, but the motivation behind acquiring it can be. Whether or not comparing assets tends to be a roadblock for you, it's one our culture crashes into all the time. Why do commercials and advertisements inundate us everywhere we look? Marketers don't spend money without reason.

Exactly how much control do you think you have over comparing your assets? In this chapter, I'll help you figure out if this is a roadblock that you often crash into, and see what you can do to avoid it.

Let's consider a familiar phrase, "Keeping up with the Joneses." It makes me think of that scene in the classic movie *National Lampoon's Christmas Vacation* when Clark makes a fool of himself trying to one-up the snooty next-door neighbors.

The popular 21st-century version of The Joneses, "*Keeping up with the Kardashians*" adds to the meaning as fashion-savvy celebrity gossip gurus seek to measure up to the hottest trends.

We've all heard the cliché, "the grass is always greener on the other side." Who hasn't fallen prey to that myth at one time or another? If we drive past our neighbor's yard, it can look pretty darn green compared to our spotty brown turf. There've been times I've let Comparison convince me to detour off course to buy some fertilizer in an attempt to remedy my landscape.

Although it's ingrained in our cultural mindset, comparing what we have to what others have is a mentality that eventually produces negative ramifications for everyone. It reinforces the lie that we are only as good as what we possess. Confusing our worth with our assets is an accident waiting to happen.

> Confusing our worth with our assets is an accident waiting to happen.

What exactly are assets, anyway? Let's learn more about them and see what costs accrue when Comparison is in control.

Money.

We use the word *asset* in a variety of contexts. An obvious usage is regarding investments, banking, retirement—anything that has to do with money. All of which can be easy to compare.

My friend, Les, shared her personal financial story on social media. At age 22, Les had over $20,000 in credit card debt, a $25,000 car loan, and a mortgage. Wanting to be free from the constraints of debt, she created a plan and acted on it. Sacrificing her social life, Les worked more than eighty hours a week and paid off everything but her mortgage. She continued to be financially free for five years, until she became a single parent. Within a year of having her baby girl, Les racked up over $25,000 in credit card debt. Again stressed, frustrated, and overwhelmed, she contemplated bankruptcy but knew deep down it wasn't her answer. She brainstormed another strategy: she cut the cable bill, changed her cell phone plan, and refinanced the mortgage. Those things alone saved her about $200 a month, but she still wasn't making a dent in her debt. Going through her budget again, line by line, she determined that her grocery bill was the only thing left to reduce. Her journey of coupon clipping began, revealing a passion (and eventually a side-hustle).

By staying focused on her destination of becoming debt-free and not comparing what she was spending with what others were buying, in a little over 36 months, she was able to pay off more than $35,000 of debt with an annual income under $50,000! Simple changes and choosing to remain in control over Comparison helped her reach her destination: financial freedom.

"Regardless of your income, you don't have to live paycheck to paycheck. Don't believe people who say you have to live a life of bills and debt, because you don't," Les encouraged in her post. "Those same people that told me that I couldn't do it as a single mother are still stagnant, and in the same position they were."

I felt inclined to share her compelling story to encourage my friend, Ted, who was drowning in debt. His reaction to her story was to say, "I wish I had a job that paid $50,000."

Ted drove straight into the roadblock of comparing assets. Instead of using Comparison to benefit him by noticing the hope and similarities that Les' story afforded, he focused on her larger salary. Ted placed himself at a lower status than Les on account of his income so he could differentiate himself from her and thereby excuse himself from doing the challenging work required to change his circumstances. By choosing not to identify with the situation, he dismissed the message and didn't have to think further about potentially taking action to get out of debt. While Comparison could've been a helpful companion, it instead became his get-away-driver toward the easy way out. Ted missed a potentially life-changing message.

Another major cost of comparing assets is inaction and missed opportunities. Ted missed the opportunity to pursue financial freedom. When you allow Comparison to take control, you're saying *take me anywhere you wish.* Comparison will take you on a detour straight to the junkyard, and once there, you feel broken down, alone, and rusted from the inside out. Trapped. Powerless. You lose sight of your real destination when Comparison has the keys—hope goes out the window.

If Ted could go in reverse and choose to take the wheel back from Comparison, he could read Les' story and decide to use Comparison to his benefit. When we claim control over how we compare our assets, Comparison can be advantageous toward helping us win in this world.

Here's how Comparison could help Ted:

1. As a single mom, Les has extra expenses and responsibility. *Ted is only responsible for himself, thus even easier for him to get out of debt. He can do this!*

2. Les is female, and she is black. Statistically, Les will only earn 83% as much as her male counterparts; as a black American, she will receive only 73% as much as her white counterparts. As a black woman, statistically, she will make only 65% as much as Ted, who is a white man.[5] *He has greater wage-earning potential. He can find a way to achieve this!*

Comparison could help Ted identify with Les' situation through revealing potential improvements and making the same choice she did: to do the work toward financial freedom and earn a debt-free life.

Possessions.

Material possessions are another form of assets we compare—house, lawn, vehicle, the latest phones and gadgets, clothes, and so on. We like our stuff and want it to measure up to others—perhaps even rise above.

Rachel Pedersen learned firsthand how much our world focuses on comparing possessions and how Comparison can attempt to detract and derail the most important aspects of life. It wasn't long ago that Rachel and her husband lived with little means. She has since built a successful social media strategy and marketing company and does well financially. A well-meaning friend (obviously under the influence of Comparison) said to her, "You should upgrade your tiny wedding ring so people know how successful you are!"

The comment left Rachel unsettled. Her "tiny" wedding ring wasn't a status symbol or an object for Comparison to flaunt; it was a special gift from her husband and a symbol of lifelong commitment.

In 2016, she posted her thoughts on Facebook, and it quickly became apparent she wasn't the only one with frustrations about living in a world where Comparison was often the driving force. Her post went viral and has had more than 247k likes and 51k shares up to this point (it's still active three years later!).

In an interview with Today.com, Rachel said that in the comments section of her post, "[M]any women were posting photos of their own rings, wanting their stories to be heard. To me, that showed a theme of physical possessions defining happiness, and a feeling of not being enough. I think a lot of women feel that."[6]

I agree with Rachel. Too many of us women get caught up in allowing possessions to dictate their worth. It's refreshing to see an example, like Rachel, who's choosing to measure up to her Innovated Identity instead of handing Comparison the wheel.

—⁓—

It's Friday night, and instead of having fun, you're on your way to meet a potential business client. All you can think about is how important it is to land this account—you need the money. You are running behind, and the closest parking spot is three blocks away from the restaurant where your prospective client asked to meet. Arriving, out of breath, you can't help but notice a classy lady emerging from her sporty black BMW® wearing a *Vogue*-worthy cocktail dress and carrying a Louis Vuitton® bag. The scent of leather seats mixed with expensive perfume lingers in the air as she hands the keys to the valet attendant and makes her way into the restaurant.

Your mind wanders for a second, wishing you had a car like that and imagining the thrill of shopping for accessories and attire without looking at a price tag. Snapping back to reality, you hope the sweat rings on your Walmart® blouse aren't visible. Once inside the restaurant, you inform the host of your reservation with someone named Alice Lane, and he escorts you to a nearby booth. A lump forms in your throat as you realize that your prospective client is none other than . . . the BMW lady.

She smiles. You return the smile, trying not to reveal the awkwardness going through your mind as Comparison takes the wheel and tells you that you don't measure up to her.

There's nothing wrong with owning and enjoying nice things, nor is it wrong to notice the things other people own. The problem arises when comparing what we do or don't have affects our mindset and, consequently, our actions.

Allowing your mind to linger too long on Comparison-controlled thoughts makes your perceived value and worth become wound up in possessions and comforts instead of focusing on who you were created to be and doing what you were designed to do. If your confidence decreases in the presence of someone who appears to be more affluent, then Comparison is in control. Why does it matter? One reason is because as your subconscious mind dwells on your prospective client's luxury car and designer apparel, Alice senses your apprehension and distraction. Your full attention isn't where it should be—on your prospect's needs and wants—rather, it's on your own.

You can be an expert in your field, providing the best service or product on the market, but if you lack confidence in yourself, your potential client is less likely to be confident in your abilities and therefore less likely to buy from you. The risk of losing a sale increases when Comparison drives your thinking—losing a sale that you should've had is leaving money on the table.

The WIN Method, which you'll soon learn, will help you regain control from Comparison in this situation with Alice. First, Weigh Your Cost. Quickly assess what Comparison will steal if you give it your wheel. Next, measure up to your Innovated Identity. Most likely you'll be reminded that material items don't measure of your worth and your focus for this meeting is simply to serve your client to the best of your ability. Lastly, Navigate Your Journey by seeing Alice as a fellow human being. Genuinely compliment her on something that you admire—perhaps share with her how stunning she looks in her dress. As women, the more that we open up with encouragement and overcome our feelings of inadequacy, the more confident we become.

Eventually, how we deal with Comparison morphs into a habit and becomes our primary thought process through which we filter information. When we are driving our vehicle, we have a clear vantage point. When Comparison takes the wheel of our life, we may inaccurately assess an individual's value according to their apparent material status.

I'm sure you've felt intimidated by people that appear to have it all. Maybe you've even harbored resentment toward them. I know I have. *Do they really need a house the size of a hotel and three sports cars?*

When we feel intimidated, or we perceive a threat, our body and mind go through chemical changes that put us in a different mode. Sometimes we don't act like our usual selves. We put our strengths and skills on the back burner and unintentionally alter our performance because of our shifted mental focus. Intimidation can express itself in many ways. People who are typically friendly and well-spoken may seem shy or antisocial, perhaps even stuttering or fumbling over their words. Some feel the need to prove themselves and act obnoxiously in an attempt to measure up.

As an employee or business owner, accounts and referrals are at stake. Prospective clients want problems solved by a confident person who is focused on serving and providing solutions—not by someone that is over-compensating, self-focused, or too distracted to perform their best. In the professional arena, allowing Comparison to have control jeopardizes your opportunities for influence and weakens the impact of your message, resulting in a loss of trust, sales, and income.

The same problem exists in our personal lives. When Comparison rules and we feel intimidated and lose confidence, we are less likely to respect our core beliefs and values. Though relationships are essential to us, we may avoid social functions, friendships, or romantic relationships because Upward Comparison causes us to think, *They have nicer things than I do so I don't measure up.*

I nearly lost out on marrying my husband for this reason. When we first met, he came across as confident and financially secure. He drove a flashy convertible sports car and took me on expensive dates. I was in unfamiliar territory and felt intimidated when focusing on his material assets compared to my humble upbringing and previous relationships.

I thought, *Who am I to live like this? Maybe this relationship isn't for me.* Thankfully, I put Comparison in its place and sent the imposter syndrome to the curb. I got to know the real Josh Vidor, married him, and we recently celebrated fifteen years of marriage!

On the contrary, we may perform a Downward Comparison. Have you ever avoided someone because they don't measure up to your lifestyle? Whether we feel judged due to what we lack or feel like someone else is less worthy of our attention due to thinking their lifestyle doesn't measure up to ours, Comparison shouldn't control our assets. Resentment and negative beliefs about others form in our minds based on what we esteem and envy. Think you do a decent job of hiding it? Don't be so sure—stinkin' thinkin' eventually leaks out, polluting our relationships and costing us interpersonally.

Let's not forget the most obvious cost of Comparison controlling our asset arena: economic loss. Staring into the Joneses' lane highlights what we don't have and what we want. Studies show the willingness to go into debt to keep up is on the rise.[7] Large or small, purchases add up, and they add up faster when Comparison handles the wheel.

Intangible Assets.

We easily recognize the tangible assets that we compare such as salaries, houses, and cars; however, there are also less obvious intangible assets. These can take us down an equally dangerous spiral of costly Comparison. These intangible assets can sneak into our subconscious and attack more stealthily than their tangible counterparts because they are often overlooked or rationalized. Let's discuss some intangible assets:

Physical Health.

We often disregard our health as an asset until it is challenged.

Joni Eareckson Tada[8] was a typical active 18-year-old who enjoyed hiking, tennis, horseback riding, and swimming. Her life changed forever when a miscalculated dive into the Chesapeake Bay resulted in a fractured neck. Joni survived, but was now paralyzed from the neck down. When she was wheeled into occupational therapy, a glance around revealed that her condition was more severe than the other patients. She learned she would never be able to use her hands again. Strong feelings of envy, depression, anger, and even suicidal thoughts began to invade her mind. It wasn't fair! Joni weighed her cost and quickly realized that despite having less physical ability than others, giving Comparison control would also cost her mental and emotional health. She *must* remain in control.

Joni couldn't change the facts: as a person with quadriplegia, her body would never work the same way it had before. Nonetheless, that wasn't her identity. She innovated her identity and navigated her journey, choosing not to use disability as an excuse. By changing her perspective, Joni's life changed—for the better.

As of today, Joni has written over forty books, recorded several musical albums, starred in an autobiographical movie of her life, earned many degrees, won countless awards, and continues to make an impact advocating for people with disabilities—all without the use of her hands or legs! Imagine the lives that would never have been impacted if Joni had allowed Comparison to drive her mind to the junkyard. Joni is a great example of how to measure up and win in a world of comparison—even when Comparison attempts to use the "it's not fair" tactic to gain control. It's true: sometimes life just isn't fair.

Relationships.

I bet you've never really thought about relationships as assets, but you probably have at least one relationship in your life that is worth more than gold. I can't imagine my life without my hubby—he is an asset to me. So are my children, parents, siblings, and many dear family members and friends. Invaluable relationships can be very satisfying. However, when we lose someone special—or simply don't have a relationship that we long for—we may feel like we don't measure up in the relational arena.

Nearly a decade ago, our family began attending a new church. It was a small congregation where everyone was kind and welcoming. Though I fit in fine, I remember my first impressions of some of the women I met and how I wished I had a friend group like theirs. They spent time together at the pool all summer, watched each other's children, went out regularly, and *did life together*. It looked so appealing from the outside, and I thought, *I wish I were a part of a group like that*.

Despite having many great friendships of my own, I still felt lonely at times and doubted the women I was comparing myself to ever experienced loneliness. I let Comparison take my mind for a drive around the block a few times when I saw those women enjoying their friendship asset.

Perhaps you've experienced Comparison's tug regarding romantic relationships. If you're single, beware: Comparison uses singleness as a tactic to make people feel left out; then it moves in to take the wheel. Seeing a couple holding hands, you may think, *Life would be so much better if I had someone by my side*.

Later, when in a romantic relationship, you look at married couples and think, *I wish I were married*.

Once married, you see couples with children and think, *If only I had children, I'd be happy like them*.

And if children come—along with the usual marital ups and downs—you realize that parenting isn't as easy and glamorous as you once thought. You glance over at that single friend of yours and think, *It must be so nice to have time, freedom, fewer responsibilities, and the ability to use the bathroom alone*.

Comparison has a way of confiscating your thoughts and emotions, wrecking contentment you should be experiencing with your current life.

Married friends, if you're beyond the honeymoon stage and have been married for any length of time, you've probably compared your marriage to other marriages. After a fight or a disappointment, you may be annoyed by social media stories of an acquaintance and her husband all cozied up on the couch sipping wine in front of the fireplace. So, you scroll on. Cat video. Cat video. And then you see it: your friend's husband surprised her with a romantic getaway for the two of them without the kids. You wish you had a snuggly spouse or one who'd think to plan a getaway on his own.

Comparison can rack up depression, discontentment, and other potentially devastating side effects to your relational tab if not controlled. This applies whether you wish you were in a relationship, or just in a different one.

Several years ago, a friend's husband decided to test-drive a younger and more exotic model woman. After taking her for a ride, he realized he also wanted the comfort of the older, reliable minivan wife that transported the family better. What began as a visual and mental comparison resulted in an out of control mentality that wrecked his marriage, damaged relationships with his children, and financially cost him an extraordinary amount in court fees. It would be tough to calculate what cost his wife and children have endured, but I can tell you it's been emotionally expensive for them. Like comedian Jay Leno from The Tonight Show says, "Marriage is grand. Divorce is about twenty grand."

The failure to claim control over Comparison is partially to blame for many major life crashes and accidents in which we find ourselves. When we appreciate the assets we have in our lives and perform the regular maintenance necessary, we are more apt to win.

Time and Other Resources.

Time is one asset we all have an equal amount of—exactly 86,400 seconds each day—yet somehow I still let Comparison trick me into thinking others have more of it than I do.

Imagine driving home from a long day at work and looking out the window to see a fit, middle-aged woman walking into a gym. It's easy to think *How in the world*

*does she find the time and energy to work out? I'm exhausted
and still have so much to do once I get home!*

Allow yourself to be vulnerable as I propose the same
tough question that I often ask myself: if you were to
map out every second of your day, are you *really* choosing
the best way to spend every single moment?

Some people use their lunch break to exercise. Still
others forgo social scrolling or evening Netflix unwind-
ing. The gal walking into the gym could be a trainer
heading to her workplace, or maybe that's how she
chooses to spend her time and energy. We are quick
to judge, but we can't logically compare how much
time a person has. Remember, it's a limited, yet equal
resource—the *utilization of it* is what we end up comparing. Though we don't know the second by second
details of any journey but our own, it's up to us to take
the wheel from Comparison and focus on our time map
and journey instead of judging others for theirs.

In all fairness, the responsibilities that consume
your time, energy, and other resources will never be an
exact replica of another's. You may have non-negotiable
details to contend with outside your control that takes
extra time—like caring for an infant, a disabled child,
or an elderly parent. Comparison may tempt you to
compare your responsibilities, making you feel better
or worse about yourself. For instance, a single parent I
know compares herself to two-parent families; she tries
to make ends meet by herself but never feels like she
has enough quality time with her kids. You may have a
chronic ailment requiring many doctor appointments,
hijacking time and energy with no productivity to show
for it.

We look out the window and see people who appear
to have it all together, while we feel our intangible assets
never measure up in this world, but that thinking is

Comparison steering. It's time to take back the wheel! You're not a victim; you have a choice. Choose to drive forward, focusing on your own lane.

Excuses.

One way to reveal if you are subconsciously comparing assets is to review your excuses. Excuses can be sneaky and challenging to uncover. It's tempting to leave them tucked away safely on Ignorance Avenue, but girlfriend, I'm telling you, you'll never experience true freedom without being brave and tackling them head on!

Let's try to discover some of your Comparison excuses. Think of something you really want that others have. Got at least one asset in mind? Now fill in the blank: *They have _____, but I can't or don't because _____.*

Whatever fills that blank is an excuse fueling Comparison to drive your journey.

Some examples are:

- I want the corporate position my friend has, but my dad isn't a CEO for a prominent company. (*I don't have the intangible assets, like connections or status*).
- If I had a big kitchen like my neighbor, I'd enjoy cooking and would make healthier meals. (*I don't have the material assets*).
- I wish I could go back to school like my coworker, but I have kids. (*I don't have the time freedom*).
- I wish my kids were on the honor roll like my sister's kids, but as a single parent I can't help them enough because I work full-time and perform the duties that two parents usually share. (*I don't have the marital relationship*).

Excuses make it easy to rationalize situations and unknowingly cover up the fact that we are giving Comparison the keys, instead of claiming control so we can win in life.

It Really Isn't Fair.

We've all said those timeless words at some time or another: "It's not fair!"

As a parent, my mind immediately goes to memories of a little kid throwing a temper tantrum over not getting what they want at the store—but these infamous three words aren't only from children. They hit home for us adults, too, and it's worth taking a closer look at what's going on when they surface.

It's true, life really isn't fair.

As you drive along your journey full of potholes and traffic, it may seem that everyone outside your window is having a lovely time lounging on the beach. You begin thinking that it's not fair you're stuck in the car traveling down the pathway of life with no vacation in sight.

Stop for a moment and ask yourself, "What is *fair*, anyway?" I find it easier to define by what it's *not*. For example, it's not fair that my friend's baby is in the hospital right now diagnosed with a brain tumor instead of being healthy like other children. It's not fair for a hardworking mom to be laid off from the job she loves, forcing her into a financial scramble. From another perspective, it's also not fair that I get to sit here freely sipping my java as I type on my laptop in a quaint air-conditioned coffee shop knowing children in other parts of the world are rummaging through garbage dumps for food in the hot sun and will never own a laptop (or even learn how to read and write).

Sure, we may see vacationers sunbathing and having a blast on their journey, but if we genuinely wanted fair for all, then we would yearn for the difficulties as well as the pleasures—and that's not what we do. Fair can be a misnomer for *I want life to be as good as it can be, and someone else's life always looks better.* Life will never be fair—sometimes we need to remind ourselves of that and be very thankful.

This ancient story helps me see fairness and Comparison from a different perspective:

Early one morning, a landowner went to the unemployment agency to find laborers for his vineyard. He hired a few, agreed to pay each a day's wage, instructed them, and sent them to work.

At nine o'clock in the morning, he returned to the unemployment agency, and, seeing people standing around without work, he hired them, too, agreeing to pay them what was right at the end of the day.

At noon, three o'clock, and five o'clock, he repeated the process.

By six o'clock, he told the supervisor to call the workers in to pay them. The laborers hired merely an hour before were called up first and received an entire day's pay! The workers that were hired early in the morning heard this and were ecstatic, assuming they'd earn more than promised since they had worked much longer than those already paid. When they went to collect their pay, the landowner gave them the same as the workers that had worked for only an hour (the amount they had agreed to that morning). "That's not fair!" they protested to the owner. "Those people only worked for an hour, but you paid them the same as us—we've been working since sunrise in the scorching heat!"

"Friends, I haven't been unfair at all," he answered. "Didn't you agree to work all day for this amount? Who cares if I wanted to pay this last worker the same as you? Is it illegal for me to do what I want with my money? Should you be jealous because I was generous to the others?"

Isn't that how we often operate? A glance out the car window becomes a stare as we focus on those who have larger salaries, more free time, or better resources, and we whine, *It's not fair*, like the morning workers. Overall, does it matter if someone else makes more money, spends their time differently, or has access to nicer things? Do others' assets change our journey at all? Only if we choose to give Comparison the ability to crash us into a ditch of discontentment.

Letting Comparison control our assets will cost us our happiness and joy. Why aren't we content with the day's wage right in front of us? It's time to stop focusing on what's out the window; instead, gaze through the front windshield ahead and focus on driving your journey.

What are some assets you have compared or fallen into discontentment about along your journey? House? Car? Money? Time? A relationship? Health? Other resources? What are some assets you recognize as a great advantage for which you can be grateful? Any road improvements made will help you cruise along a smoother journey toward freedom.

Do you currently have control over Comparison regarding your assets? Rate your level of control on a scale of 1 to 10.

(full control) 1 2 3 4 5 6 7 8 9 10 (no control)

CHAPTER THREE

The Appearances Roadblock:
They look better than I do.

Appearance (n)
The way that someone or something looks.

In our looks-obsessed world, this roadblock needs the
least introduction. A simple glance in the mirror reveals
that you look different than other people. What's sad is
how we tend to scorn our differences instead of celebrate
them. Do you believe you're in control of whether you
compare your personal appearance to how other people
look? Keep reading and learn why your beliefs from the
mirror are not always as they appear, and how you can
finally measure up.

Appearance happens to be the roadblock that I've
crashed into most often. Certain aspects of my physical
appearance fail to measure up to what I envision they

should. A glimpse at a magazine cover with an attractive woman with flawless filtered beauty reminds me of where my body fails to comply with society's standards—and thus, the standards I claimed for myself. I've always longed for a darker complexion with that bronzed-skin glow, so I'd get a spray tan to not feel like the pastiest woman around. After nursing two infants and experiencing a major gravitational change, I felt like there was no way I could measure up in the boob department. So, I chose to have a breast augmentation as a surprise to my husband for our 6th wedding anniversary. I did these things to measure up.

Image comparison begins early for females, and it's based around the messages that our world sends us. As a child, you were probably given a thin, curvy, voluptuous Barbie doll as a toy. I remember brushing Barbie's straight blonde hair, longing for it to replace my wavy red locks. While many females have been conditioned to want Barbie's frame, if this Mattel-made icon were a full size to-scale adult, she would be 5'9" tall, weigh 110 lbs., have a 39" bust, an 18" waist, 33" hips, and a size three shoe. Her BMI would be right smack in the anorexic range.[9] That is the image young girls begin using as a target goal: long slender legs, generous thigh gap, perfect hourglass figure, large beaming blue eyes, lots of makeup and flawless skin—an unnatural combination. Barbie has been the impossible standard since she debuted in 1959, creating an unstable foundation for never measuring up. She's been the recipe of unmet expectations for generations of women.

There's another side of the image-comparison dilemma, too. While we may not feel like we measure up in this world physically, we observe others who do not either. Ever looked at someone through the eyes of

Comparison and thought they didn't visually measure up for one reason or another?

"Makeup would hide her acne and minimize her big nose."

"She really should lose some weight."

"That distracting mole on her face needs to go."

Regardless of which direction, when we hand Comparison the keys to the appearance arena of our life, we end up off course. Whether we detour to the land of arrogance or, the opposite direction, the land of low self-esteem, the cost of living is astronomical in both regions, and the conditions aren't good.

So why do we let Comparison take us there?

Power and Success.

Appearance has played a part in human history for as long as we can remember. Fashion and image have been an important part of each historical era. Think back to your high school history books showcasing the fancy Renaissance dresses from the seventeenth century. Or consider the ridiculous corsets in the late nineteenth century. I can't help but wonder if Adam and Eve got caught up in whether they looked good in their animal skins.

When talking about appearance, the topic of weight comes up often. Did you know that up until around 1900, it was a universal symbol of beauty to be what we consider in modern culture as obese? Back then, a plump frame signified attractiveness, wealth, and power for men and was a sign of beauty and fertility for women. Thin women were at a disadvantage in marriageability. We know by today's mainstream media that the socially desired body mass has since flip-flopped, but the power struggle with Comparison and appearance remains unchanged.

Famines were common before the 19th century, so consuming enough food to have extra padding signified success. Today, roughly 100 years later, our ability to get food has improved with technology and transportation. If we are reading this book, we most likely have access to everything we need and much of what we want. Today it costs more money, time, and self-control to maintain a non-obese body weight, but we still compare ourselves like they did in the 1900s. *Do I measure up to society's standards? Do I look good enough to get what I need and want in life?*

The Opposite Sex.

Gender relevance and sex appeal are also rooted in why we tend to give Comparison control regarding our appearance and seek to measure up to our female counterparts.

Historically, a woman didn't provide for herself. Marriage determined a lady's social standing, provision, and fate. As she competed against other women, her looks were a crucial component in attracting the affection of a successful man and winning him over.

The idea of a trophy wife, married for physical appearance, makes me cringe—we are so much more than our appearance and should be appreciated as such. Thankfully, times have changed in many ways, yet shows like *The Bachelor* and *The Bachelorette,* make me question how far we've actually come.

Especially in Western culture, there's been a shift and women have gained more economic independence. They are less dependent on a husband for security, so this should provide less pressure for competition. Why then does Comparison seem to be steadily increasing in control over us? As technology increases, the ability to retreat from the outside world decreases. A 2015 study reports that 90 percent of young adults use social media, up from a mere 12 percent in 2005. That's a 78 percent increase in a little over a decade![10] We are constantly exposed to images, media, and advertisements flaunting what successful people look like, how our appearance is related to our acceptance, and the notion that if we don't jump on the bandwagon with the rest of the world of Comparison, we will never measure up to what we are supposed to be. There's no respite or escape. And, of course, we want to measure up.

Making Decisions.

We often associate using sex appeal to achieve our wants or needs, be it a spouse, a job, or an award. What are some other reasons we compare our appearance?

In Chapter One, we referenced Social Comparison Theory and how we are innately driven to compare. We want to figure out accurate self-evaluations, reduce uncertainty, and differentiate ourselves. By comparing our appearance, we are searching for something to be a benchmark of where we stand and a measurement to help us define who we are. Our minds are always looking for the path of least resistance so we can make quick choices and decisions based on the information we collect and internalize.

Let's create an example and call her Amy. Amy found a great fitness series to stream so she can work out to lose some extra weight. She wants to figure out how often she should exercise to achieve the weight loss she desires. The trainer on the videos is an attractive young woman with no visible body fat. If Amy benchmarks with the trainer, here are two potential thoughts that Comparison will give Amy to choose from:

1. I want to achieve the same results the instructor is enjoying. I'm not where I want to be yet, and it's going to take time and effort to achieve the results I want for myself.

   I'll work out five days a week!

2. Gosh, look at her! I don't measure up—I could exercise every day and still never look that good—why try?

   I'll work out when I feel like it.

We know which choice is easier. Amy gets to choose her mindset and whether she'll utilize Comparison properly to her benefit, or give it control over her. You get the same choice as Amy: will you use Comparison to motivate you, or let it discourage you?

Personal Trauma.

Personal trauma can create an appearance roadblock. One of my best friends in middle school was verbally abused. Her mom repeatedly told her that her nose was too big, and she was too ugly to go out of the house without makeup. She was required to curl her hair and apply ample amounts of makeup every day for school. I remember her being terrified by what would happen if her mom found out that she didn't have time to do her hair.

Even favoritism can cause trauma. I sat at a restaurant listening to Jean, who was 22 at the time, share about her upbringing and how it still affected her today. Jean had a twin sister, Heather, who was slimmer, a better athlete, and got better grades than she did. Her mother outwardly favored Heather and told Jean she couldn't measure up. Jean admitted how, even today, she struggles to push herself to excel. We are more apt to hand our keys to Comparison when it's been drilled into our psyche that we're never enough. Siblings—especially twins or multiples—stand a higher chance of being affected by Comparison. There could be the smart one, the athletic one, or the pretty one. In the town where I grew up, three sisters close in age were often compared by their looks. A guy friend once said, "Every daughter gets more attractive—their parents should have another, and she'd be perfect." I can only hope that the firstborn daughter never heard this hurtful remark.

As exemplified by Cherie's story in Chapter One, physical betrayal is a trauma that can also be a catalyst for Comparison controlling our appearances. Similarly, when a woman discovers her partner viewing pornography, she often internalizes the on-screen comparisons and feels like she doesn't measure up visually or sexually. Feeling too large in certain areas, or not large enough in others, she moves over and gives Comparison the wheel, thinking, *My body and appearance can't satisfy my partner; I'm not sexy enough.* Though lack of contentment with a partner's appearance doesn't necessarily correlate with the reasons behind pornography addiction according to Dr. Kurt Smith, LMFT, LPCC, AFC,[11] it's still difficult for the betrayed partner to separate the visual and relational aspect. Allowing Comparison to take control is how some deal with their insecurities.

Overconfidence.

It's wonderful to be confident with who you were created to be and satisfied with how you were created
to appear, but vanity doesn't look pretty on anybody.
Overconfidence or arrogance can be a negative result
of allowing Comparison to steer your life. While some
people may be just plain vain, acting out in arrogance
often is the outcome of feeling inferior. An inflated
ego can be a defense mechanism. It enables a person to
judge and reject others before they can themselves feel
rejected. Overconfidence is a preemptive punch that
saves people from feeling knocked out in life.

I want to differentiate between mere overconfidence
and personality disorders. People with Narcissistic
Personality Disorder (NPD) have an inflated sense of
self-worth, a great need for admiration, and they feel
no empathy toward others. Those with NPD and other
mental health disorders require professional help, and it
would be beneficial for family members or those close
to someone with these disorders to receive counseling
as well.[12] Consequently, children who are raised by
someone with a personality disorder (especially NPD)
are more likely to struggle with Comparison regarding
their appearance.

Money.

Keeping up with appearances has a potentially serious
cost that can spend you out of house and home when
Comparison is navigating.

Hair. Skin. Nails. Face. Clothing. Fitness. Surgery.
The list goes on forever.

As of 2019, the global beauty industry is a $532
billion-dollar industry and is projected to grow to over

$806 billion by 2023.[13] According to a survey commissioned by Groupon in 2017, the average makeup shopping trip is $43 per person, and the average American woman spends $15,000 in her lifetime—on beauty products alone.[14] If you had the option of owning a car or wearing makeup throughout your life, which would you choose?

It's not just beauty products; the average woman spends $225,360 in her lifetime on her overall appearance[15]. Looking how we think the world wants us to look can cost us a lot of hard-earned moolah! I doubt we'd invest in this like we do if we didn't feel the need to look good when compared to others.

The Deserted Island Test.

To be clear, not all image-related expenses are due to Comparison-controlled spending. Some decisions could take place regardless of whether Comparison, or ourselves, were navigating our life. For instance, in addition to making our bodies look good, physical fitness is also a health benefit and functions as a stress-reducer. Here's a quick mental exercise to help you identify whether you're innocently acting according to your comfort and preference, or you are Comparison-driven and trying to measure up to what others think. I call it The Deserted Island Test.

Ask yourself these questions:

If I was the only person living on a deserted island and no one else would ever see me, would I still buy _____? (process through all of your products)

Would I still do _____? (process through your appearance-related actions)

Would I be concerned about _____? (process through
the thoughts and concerns associated with image)

Some of the things I would still buy would be tooth-
paste, moisturizer, and lip gloss—I cannot stand dry lips.
What I'd still do is exercise and cut my hair—in fact,
if it was a warm island, I'd probably cut most of it off.
What I'd still be concerned about would be sun exposure, because my fair skin tends to burn very quickly.

A brief list of what I would *not* do is apply makeup,
style my hair, get a spray tan, get breast implants, wear
jewelry or fancy clothes, and I'd definitely ditch the high
heels! All of those things would be pointless.

I do some things to measure up to what society
implies will make me look more attractive. But why? Do
I believe I will be more accepted? Will people like me
more? Is my worth only as good as the opinion others
have of me? Truth be told, if people's like for me at the
grocery store is based on whether I styled my hair or
have a case of bed head, that's their loss.

Nonetheless, I don't live on a deserted island, and I
still actively do many of those things. And yes, they do
result in extra money, time, energy, and sometimes even
pain (those darn cute shoes!), but those are the costs
I'm ok with. It's also important to notice that, since
we don't live on a deserted island, having an overall
orderly appearance can be a reflection of our character
in our society, thus affecting our ability to obtain a job.
Regardless, it's good to be aware of our Comparison
tendencies and from where they stem.

Joy. Happiness. Contentment.

Have you ever felt someone staring you up and down with eyes of Comparison? Perhaps they see you as competition, or they're jealous? These vibes can be sensed when someone doesn't like you because you're somehow perceived as a threat to them.

My husband, Josh, recently reminded me of such an example.

Josh had been working for a relatively young company that was doing very well. It seemed that the young owner had all she could want, as they were receiving awards, growing, and expanding massively.

At the company Christmas party, I was making small talk with Meredith the company owner. Immediately, I sensed that this lady really didn't care for me. I confided my feelings with Josh later as we left the party in our fancy dressed-up attire. He couldn't imagine why I would think that Meredith had a problem with me and brushed it off as a mere misunderstanding or possibly my imagination—but I knew. Something was strange in her demeanor toward me.

For the next year's Christmas party, I decided to dress less flashy due to feeling awkward from the previous year's negative glances from Meredith. "I don't want any bad feelings," I said to Josh, "and I have this hunch that she didn't like me because of my appearance." He laughed it off as unnecessary and told me to wear whatever I wanted. I followed my female intuition and wore a modest, low-key black dress.

Meredith was there greeting guests as we entered the banquet hall. We walked up to share our congratulations on the company's great year. She leaned in to reciprocate the hug I offered, but stopped midway as she looked me up and down and said, "Somehow, you always manage to show me up."

My husband heard the awkward comment and was attempting to scrape his jaw off of the floor as I also stood there speechless. My intuition had been spot-on. Ultimately, it didn't matter what dress I wore or how kind I was. Comparison had the keys to Meredith's life, and nothing I could do would change the resentment that was internally driving her to react this way.

After I recovered from the shock of the moment, I began to feel compassion for her. Here was a woman in the prime of her life, running a successful company, married with young children, who owned an expensive house, luxury SUV, and whatever else she wanted, and yet, she was letting Comparison drive her down the detour of Discontentment. Had Meredith chose to Weigh the Cost of Comparison to see what it was costing her, innovate her identity to recognize and own her personal value, and then Navigate her Journey to avoid the potholes of Comparison, she would be so much happier!

When Comparison takes control, our reputation may suffer as those around us notice the adverse effects and lose respect for us. What should be joyful moments—like celebrating Christmas and company achievements—are turned into moments of misery and bitterness because the focus centered on comparing appearances. We may create enemies in our minds instead of forming friendships or beneficial business alliances.

Relationships.

I wish I could say I've never had a Meredith moment and given Comparison the keys, but that would be a big fat lie.

A few years ago, I was assisting on a team hosting a large international business conference. I noticed a new lady I hadn't met, who was gorgeous with a beautiful, radiant smile and a gentle demeanor. I instantly felt Comparison's controlling thoughts revving inside my mind, though I didn't understand those feelings at the time. To this day, I still couldn't tell you what threat I was perceiving! There was no competition for anyone or anything. Nothing was at stake, and yet, instead of being my naturally welcoming self, I gave Comparison control and avoided her so I didn't have to deal with those uncomfortable feelings. Looking back I realize how selfish I was.

The next year I walked into the team welcome dinner and guess who was sitting there with an open seat next to her? The gorgeous gal from the previous year. Since I'd been heavily researching for this very topic, I knew I had to claim control over Comparison and redeem the situation.

"Is anyone sitting here?" I asked her as I introduced myself.

Her name was Dee—she and I hit it off like friends who had known each other forever. We enjoyed working alongside each other that weekend, and before our time ended, I knew one step remained for me to completely put Comparison in its place. I needed to confess to Dee how I had snubbed her the previous year. After vulnerably sharing my prior year's actions and asking for her forgiveness, she opened up that she, too, had experienced the same appearance-based Comparison takeover toward me—and it had the same effect on her!

It goes to show how we never know what others are feeling or experiencing, and we also never know what a moment of authenticity and opening up might uncover.

I'll never know what Dee and I missed out on the previous year—what positive interactions could have taken place if we had taken control over Comparison earlier? Isn't it crazy how something as silly as physical appearance can change our usual behavior, hinder us from forming relationships, and cause us to act so selfishly?

Hopelessness.

If you feel like you will never measure up, what's the point in navigating toward your destination? Who cares if Comparison takes the wheel when it seems as if everyone else is succeeding toward their finish line and you're going nowhere fast? Hopelessness is a real place, and Comparison will drive you straight there.

As a brain cancer survivor, 11-year-old Bethany Thompson had overcome so much, yet the effects of Comparison led to tragedy. Though Bethany beat cancer, the tumor had damaged a nerve, leaving her with a crooked smile. Students teased and bullied her due to her abnormal appearance until the afternoon she lost control and couldn't take it anymore. The bullying became too much for her to bear, so she ended her young life.

Comparison most likely played a part in both sides of this sad story: for Bethany *and* her antagonists. Bethany didn't feel like she was measuring up in appearance and typically bullies hurt others because they're hurting inside and don't feel good about themselves. According to a study of more than 10,000 young people in the UK aged 12-20,[16] the real reason a bully abuses others isn't because of their victims uniqueness, rather it is because they are hurting and crying out for attention. However, the person being bullied often internalizes the pain. We need to work hard to teach our youth to take control over Comparison and not allow what others say or do to affect their perceived identity.

Comparison is costly. In this case, Bethany lost her very life. The rest of the world missed out on the potential that she never got to live out. Bethany's parents experienced heartache beyond words, and the young bullies who taunted Bethany likely suffered guilt and shame because of their terrible actions.

The topic of suicide is important—we need to camp out here for a minute. We can't simply write it off as being selfish or blame mental illness as the sole cause. If you have experienced feelings of hopelessness when Comparison was driving your thought patterns, or have been the victim of comparison expressed by others (bullying), you know there's a fine line between making rational choices and giving in to irrational thoughts.

As I write this chapter, another student in my local community took his life—a high school freshman who was relentlessly bullied. While I didn't know him, my heart aches anytime I hear of someone being bullied—especially to the point of feeling they don't measure up enough to continue living in this world. While youth aren't the only ones feeling hopeless and taking their lives, they do have a greater chance to follow through because their brains aren't as developed in the area of rational thinking. We've got to do something about this. How can we be a catalyst for change? By claiming control over Comparison in our own lives, we can make a difference. We can be role models, giving permission for others to claim control of their lives. We can take it a step further and be an example: refrain from comparing or judging others.

It's imperative to take a stand for those who are bullied—youth or adults—when they don't yet have the courage to stand up for themselves. If you are unable to stand up for the person in the moment, find a way to intercede and help. Be known as a person who is approachable and available.

> Be known as a person who is approachable and available.

A form of bullying that many are ignorant to is gossip. Engaging in conversations about others that could be potentially hurtful or derogatory is wrong. Kindly call it out and put an end to any conversations that take a turn toward gossip. Instead, speak words of encouragement, affirming others, and let people know they are beautiful and valued. Reach out and talk to the lady hanging her head as she waits for the bus. Save a seat for the quiet, quirky coworker who sits alone at lunch. Everyone can use more kindness. Remember, it's not only the outcasts who feel the weight of Comparison; everyone does at some point. Sometimes it's you, sometimes it's me, and sometimes it's the celebrities we see on TV.

The acclaimed actress Meryl Streep overheard a producer calling her "ugly" in Italian when she was auditioning for a role in *King Kong*. Her response was classic. She responded in fluent Italian, "I'm very sorry that I'm not as beautiful as I should be, but you know—this is it. This is what you get."[17]

Ms. Streep chose not to measure up with the stereotypical image society was asking of her, and she didn't give in to Comparison's temptation to give up. Instead, she embraced her appearance and went on to succeed by being who she was created to be and doing what she was designed to do. It paid off. She has been nominated for nearly thirty Golden Globe awards—winning eight—and has had numerous Oscar nominations with three wins, as well as many other awards throughout her career.[18]

It never works out well when we try to be someone we weren't created to be, so why waste time, money, and effort? When we catch ourselves looking at another person to figure out how good (or not-so-good) we look, it's time to take a step back and re-evaluate whether we have control over comparing our appearance and image, or if Comparison has control over us. It's time we start working as hard to fit comfortably in our genes as we do to fit into our jeans.

Do you currently have control over Comparison regarding your appearance? Rate your level of control on a scale of 1 to 10.

(full control) 1 2 3 4 5 6 7 8 9 10 (no control)

CHAPTER FOUR

The Achievements Roadblock: They perform better than I do.

Achievement (n)
A thing done successfully, typically by effort, courage, or skill.
Synonyms: attainment, accomplishment, fulfillment, implementation, execution, performance

From an early age, we are taught to accomplish. We are encouraged to work hard to achieve our goals, told that the sky is the limit, and pushed to reach the next milestone. It's no wonder we attempt to find our worth by comparing our accomplishments to those around us. Do you find yourself comparing your achievements to everybody else's? Keep reading to learn whether you are stuck comparing, and if you are, how to stop.

Most of us are familiar with beauty pageants, like the *Miss America* competition. The glamour and glitz capture our attention as beautiful young women cross the stage in their gowns and heels, carrying their poise, confidence, and accomplishment—on the outside. But behind those pearly white smiles and fake eyelashes, they're each asking themselves questions such as, "Will I be the one to take the crown home? What if I don't finish in the top three? Do I measure up?"

Pageants never interested me and I would never have seen myself in a competition of that nature. However, several years ago I was nominated by a few friends and found myself participating in the *Mrs. International Pageant.* Though I had no expectation of winning the crown, I did my best to take it seriously and put in the work. I knew that a title could be a nice resume-builder with some other benefits, but what sold me on entering the pageant was the prospect of personal growth. It was time to step out of my comfort zone.

Despite my lack of pageant experience, when all nine of us contestants were together for the first time, I knew which one would take home the crown. It was no surprise to me when she won first place. What did catch me off guard, however, was the winner of another award: the fitness award.

Before the winner was announced, there were whispers backstage this award belonged to me. Exercise was an important part of my lifestyle, and I had worked hard to get in great shape. To be fully transparent, the idea of winning that particular award was *very* appealing to me. Of course, who wouldn't love to walk away from that experience with an external achievement—as well as the internal growth?

We all huddled together behind the curtain in anticipation. A couple of women tapped me and winked. My heart raced as the announcer spoke, "And the winner of the fitness award is. . ."

Not me.

The award went to an amazing lady—a true sweetheart who was gorgeous inside and out. She was indeed on a great fitness journey of her own—one that quickly progressed after the pageant in part to winning this award—but her physical results weren't as outwardly visible at that time. *I am more deserving of that award,* I thought.

I had a choice to make. Was I going to concede to Comparison's taunt and compare the winner's new status to my lack of acknowledgment? Or would I continue to be thrilled achieving personal growth and genuinely celebrate this wonderful woman and her award? I won't lie; I struggled at first, but after weighing my cost, I knew that bitterness wasn't what I wanted. I measured up to my Innovated Identity— jealousy wasn't part of the real me. Then, I navigated my journey by genuinely congratulating the winner. I put Comparison back where it belonged—along with the accompanying feelings of jealousy and pride.

Imagine driving down the road of life, straining to focus on your destination. It's nearly visible in the distance when a car zooming past in the next lane distracts you. Watching as it maneuvers effortlessly around curves and potholes, you're left behind, staring at the "26.2" sticker on the back and a vanity plate that read "NUMBR 1."

You know nothing about the driver or where they're headed, but a surge of rivalry and competitiveness runs through your veins. You accelerate until you catch up, and notice she is a local celebrity. She glances back over at you, smiles, nods, and speeds ahead. Trailing closely behind, the Channel 10 News chases her, wanting an interview—while fans and followers putter behind, praising her every swerve.

The experience leaves you feeling slow, incompetent, and insignificant. Why does *she* have all the skills, status, and achievements, and you're left to eat *her* dust? Thoughts creep into your mind like, *I'm not as fast as she is, not as successful, I don't have any followers, and I don't have a bumper sticker, but if I did, it would say 0.0. I'm never good enough.* You slide to the passenger's seat and let Comparison take your wheel.

You were so close to *your* destination, yet that glance out the window turned into a stare—so you never made it there. That's what happens when we focus on others' achievements instead of our destination.

Back to our car metaphor, when driving a vehicle, we must look around occasionally to be aware of our surroundings and ensure the safety of ourselves, other drivers, and pedestrians. Similarly, in life we should see, recognize, and appreciate the talents, abilities, and contributions others bring to the world through their journey. Still, it's downright dangerous when a glance turns into a gaze.

> We steer where we stare.

We lose sight of the road in front of us by focusing on others and comparing our achievements to theirs. As you've learned, Comparison, in and of itself, isn't detrimental; it's when we give Comparison control of our wheel that we are destined to crash. Never forget—we steer where we stare.

Focus forward on your own destination and limit the time you allow your eyes to spend looking out the side windows.

Competition: The Good and Bad

Working hard and desiring to be your best is admirable. In sports, athletes are encouraged to do whatever possible within the rules to beat their opponents. In business, we admire and reward the companies that stand out from the rest. After all, that's what competition is, right? It's comparing how you're doing with someone or something else to see how much improvement is needed to excel. As we discussed previously, Comparison in and of itself isn't harmful. In fact, we learned how it can be beneficial when used correctly.

Comparison is necessary for competition. Without it, we'd be without progress that we've come to appreciate— including many great inventions we take for granted today. Consider the competition between Microsoft and Apple that continually brings us the technology innovation we enjoy both as businesses and consumers. As the two companies compete to be the first to release the latest innovations, everyone benefits.

Can you imagine what would happen to entertainment as we know it if competition didn't exist? There would be no Olympics, that's for sure! Take a peek on YouTube of Olympic gymnasts' from the 1950s and, alternatively, from recent years. You'll be amazed at the improvements people have made as they push their personal limits and perform better than their predecessors. This is one example demonstrating Comparison's proper place in our world, though it is our responsibility to keep it in perspective.

So how does our everyday constructive competitiveness morph into an all-out demolition derby? It's when we give Comparison the wheel and focus on the achievements of our competition—we lose focus on the reason we are competing in the first place. All too often, people veer way off-course and wind up in the path of destruction.

American professional road racing cyclist and triathlete, Lance Armstrong, is a prime example. Lance won several world racing championships and was on his way to the top—even stage four cancer didn't keep him down. He still needed to prove himself against a few competitors before he could claim to be the best cyclist. Sadly, Lance chose to break organizational guidelines by using performance-enhancing drugs to beat his competition and get ahead.

He never got to achieve that number one spot. In 2012, as a result of using banned substances, he was stripped of his former titles and barred from future Olympic sports for life. Lance gave Comparison the handlebars and focused more on achieving a winning status than reaching the destination that was meant for him. The cost was astronomical: the loss of his career and passion, broken relationships, a marred reputation, and a $100 million lawsuit.

Had Lance followed the rules and foregone the drugs, who knows if he would have surpassed his opponents, but I am confident that he would still be remembered as an amazing athlete and would measure up to who he was created to be. Instead, he's infamous for the biggest doping scandal in cycling history.[19]

Impact.

Jordan and Michelle were business partners running a successful small marketing company. Though their business was doing well, they still tended to gaze longer than they should at larger marketing companies, wishing they had prominent clients like their competitors had.

A professional sports team approached Jordan with a potential million-dollar business opportunity. While she wasn't entirely confident that the two of them could handle the contract and still serve their current clients well, Comparison reminded her that this would be their big break to measure up to their competition. So, they sold the deal and signed the contract.

It didn't take long for the partners to realize their new contract brought on an immense workload and expectations that were beyond the capability of their small firm. Their established clients were falling by the wayside. Dissatisfied with the outcome, the sports team retracted their project offer—along with the million-dollar opportunity. The financial setback put an enormous strain on the partnership, eventually resulting in the closure of their company.

Comparison-based decisions can come at an exorbitant cost. The impact of driving head-on into the roadblock of achievements proved to be fatal for Jordan and Michelle's company. Their decision to give Comparison the wheel had a trickledown effect for their clients in that they now had to invest time and energy into finding a new marketing company. We rarely see the full impact our thoughts and decisions have on ourselves as well as others—whether positive or negative.

Our achievements and accomplishments have the potential to be a broad platform from which we can impact our world. You possess innate abilities and gifts that exist to help you reach your destination and achieve your purpose. Though I can readily identify talent in others, I'm often oblivious to my own. And when I know my gifts, sometimes I downplay them. I bet you do the same. It's common to look at the driver in the next lane and think, *Her life journey is more appealing. I'm nothing special.*

Peering into the next lane causes us to lose momentum and lose sight of our significance. We've all felt small, less-than, or worthless when observing someone else who is super-productive, climbing the status ladder faster, or who appears to perform better than us.

As drivers, we lose sight of the incredible power we possess behind the wheel and the risk that comes when we allow ourselves to be distracted. Do you also know that your life is a vessel of power? Never forget that you have limitless potential and value. Don't allow Comparison to distract you from living in it.

Like you, I've been guilty of staring out the window and forgetting my capabilities and what I was created to offer the world. Recently, I was reminded of the importance of taking positive action, regardless of how small or insignificant it may seem. Soon after that, I overcame the intimidation of posting videos of myself on social media. Though there were messages I knew I was meant to share, I was worried about what people would think of me. Thoughts cruised through my head. *What if I look stupid? Why would anyone want to watch my videos when there are plenty of other people who post better stuff?* I allowed Comparison to keep me from navigating forward because I was intimidated by the possibility of people on the other side of the screen judging me.

Then it hit me: *Who cares?* Who cares what people think of me? Who cares if my videos aren't edited or refined like someone else's, or if my messages aren't as profound? Who cares if I only have a few viewers while others have a few million?

If only one person benefits from my video, wasn't it worth it? I came to grips with the fact that what other people think about me is none of my business. This realization was freeing.

I kicked Comparison out and took back my rightful spot in the driver's seat.

> What other people think about me is none of my business.

Now I post videos regularly and some have made a significant impact. I may see myself as merely talking for a few minutes, but in reality, I'm doing much more. I'm sharing my passion, encouragement and inspiration. I'm utilizing my ability to speak and my knowledge of how to operate a smartphone to post to social media. I'm acting on the simple things and focusing on what I can achieve right now.

On my drive to the gym this morning, the beautiful sunrise summoned me to pull over and record a quick video despite the freezing 15 degrees Fahrenheit temperature. Comparison-controlled thinking crept in as I pictured how dumb I'd look chattering through a video with a Rudolph-red nose with a message that probably wasn't incredibly significant anyhow. Recognizing Comparison's voice, I decided to fight it, take control, and pull over to shoot the video. The topic was *How to deal when life gets tough*. I posted it and went on my way to the gym.

Later that morning, I received a message from a woman across the globe that said, "Thank you, Renee, for your video! I am dealing with leukemia again . . . and soon I will have to do the transplant, your words were precious! A big hug!"

Tears brimmed in my eyes, reminding me to clean my windshield more often to get rid of the Comparison residue blurring my vision and keeping me from my destination. I've received many similar affirmations over the past few years reminding me that my videos do matter— even if they're unrefined and authentically imperfect.

It's sobering to know lives have been impacted due to making the choice to take control from Comparison in this area of achievements.

This concept goes much further than my videos. I'm sure you've been impacted by a book. How about a song? I certainly have. People say that a book helped save their marriage or a song jolted them to their senses, and they refrained from committing suicide. What if the author, songwriter, musician, singer, publisher, or producer of that content had thought *someone else does it better* and that particular book or song was never released? Marriages are thriving today, and a person is breathing today because someone chose to win control over Comparison! That person of impact could be you.

How many opportunities have been missed because of simple Comparison-based decisions that we brush off as unimportant? We can never know the extent of our impact. That's humbling.

Much of what we do (or don't do) matters, regardless of our title, status, audience, or affirmations. What are you refraining from doing, or not giving your all to because you're focusing on the pace of drivers in the next lane? It's time to look ahead.

The Cost of Time.

Last year I attended a conference where I met a lady named Erin who was in the process of writing a fiction book. When I asked how far she had progressed, she said, "Not as far as I should have."

Erin had been excitedly writing her story until a non-fiction author she admired released his first fiction book and it was terrific—she felt intimidated. She began doubting her abilities and thinking she couldn't measure up to the talent of the other author. Her writing came to a screeching halt when she gave Comparison the keys.

"I've lost a lot of time" Erin said. "If I would've kept focused on the book inside of me instead of wasting so much time comparing my ideas to his, I'd probably be finished!" Comparison has the power to slam on the brakes and keep us from traveling toward our destination—but only when we allow it in the driver seat.

Much time is wasted by focusing on others' spotlight moments and achievements instead of steadily following our map toward success. Innocently scrolling social media, allowing our minds to wander off course when our time is spent better elsewhere, we are sucked into comparing our accomplishments to another's. It consumes our productivity. I've personally observed this when I've become obsessed with learning about another person. Perhaps you've also misspent your time, focusing too much on others who intimidate you—a colleague, athletic opponent, business competitor, fellow contestant, or someone in a group you've joined. Social media and Google become the source for information on this perceived competition—every keynote given, score earned, or review received. Hyper-focused on the other person's performance, we subconsciously ask ourselves: *Am I as good as she/he is? Can I keep up with or surpass her/him?*

Do a person's achievements actually determine how good a person is or their worth? Not at all. And, why do we want to keep up or surpass someone else in their journey? We have our own to navigate. The fastest way to get from one point to another is a straight line. When our eyes fixate on something, we head in the direction of what we are looking at—our car veers in the direction of our fixation. When we look to the side instead of driving in the direction of our destination, we steer off course, often resulting in a collision. If you've ever been in an accident, you know how much time is wasted.

Be aware of the time you spend focusing on outside factors. As you drive along your journey, follow the path toward your destination and stay in your lane.

We All Have Abilities and Significance.

Ever felt like everyone else has amazing abilities, and you're, well, *ordinary?* Driving our daily route can become quite mundane. A friend I was working alongside the other day tried to explain something technical to me (his first mistake), and after many failed attempts (I'm not very tech-savvy), he said, "Sometimes I forget that not everyone knows what I know about this."

As we grow accustomed to our knowledge, routine tasks, and regular accomplishments, our appreciation for what we do and why we do it diminishes. This leads to feeling undervalued. We play small—second guessing our abilities—especially when we focus out the window and think, *I'm not as good.*

Stay-at-home moms are familiar with the feeling of mundane days and lack of appreciation. A magazine cover featuring Angelina Jolie once got me thinking, "Why am I *just* a stay-at-home mom wiping noses, changing diapers, grocery shopping, cooking, and taxiing kids around all day while she's doing all those things— with more children than I have—and also traveling, acting, being a humanitarian, and who knows what all else?"

Comparison is everywhere. It's on your television screen, on your smart phone, in your church, and in the grocery store aisle. You can't escape it, but you *can* claim control over it.

To my mom readers: We often forget that staying home with children is a remarkably vital task with amazing payoffs and one that needs and deserves more recognition. The vast skill set necessary for this role—things like patience, attention to detail, creativity, management, human resources, and super-human energy—outweigh those needed for many other job descriptions! I've talked to moms who are financially able to stay home yet choose to work and pay daycare or a babysitter because they feel incapable of the stay-at-home-mom role. We all have our capacity and our strengths, let's stop comparing and judging others for theirs . . . and start celebrating ours.

Engineers, teachers, and parents are essential. Working in a factory machining a tiny part that makes our cars operate safely is a necessary ability. Without food workers, you couldn't buy your sandwich at Chik-fil-A®. The janitor at your office and the person collecting your weekly garbage from your home are often overlooked, yet they, and their achievements, are important. So is the pilot who flies you to visit your parents, and the doctor who helped you get well.

Every honest job is valuable, and every single human being has valuable gifts, talents, and abilities to offer the world. People are born with intrinsic significance and have the innate capability to achieve and measure up. Whether or not they choose to exercise their abilities, well, that's their choice.

You may ask, what about the mentally or physically disabled person who needs 24/7 care—what value do they bring to society? They, too, have abilities, even if they're less definable in our finite perspective.

In her book *Voiceless,*[20] author Angela Dee shares the story of her son, Spencer, who was a typical kid until age six when he contracted a virus that attacked his brain, changing his life forever. Spencer can no longer walk, talk, or perform tasks our society perceives to be productive, and yet, his life has impacted many. Angela shares how Spencer has always had a special connection with God and the supernatural, which has inspired many. He's also taught people to fight relentlessly and never give up, just as he's been doing for many years. It's futile to compare Spencer's life to yours, mine, or anyone else's because we are all on different roads leading to unique destinations. If someone with such major challenges as Spencer has impacted so many without even speaking a word, then what's your excuse? Our significance isn't measured by what we *do* but by who we *are*.

Here's another way you can utilize Comparison's beneficial qualities: occasionally take inventory of your achievements and capabilities and assess whether you're using them to their full potential. Take some

> Our significance isn't measured by what we *do* but by who we *are*.

time to identify and acknowledge your specific talents, strengths, and gifts you've been given. Being careful not to let Comparison drive you down Arrogance Alley, celebrate your personal accomplishments and the miles you've traveled thus far during your life journey.

Your abilities and achievements are unique to you.

The only beneficial reason for comparing them is for inspiration and ideation to continue utilizing and improving the strengths, skills, and talents with which you were created.

Do you have the ability to speak? Then use your voice to convey an important message.

Can you walk? Then get up and visit someone.

Are you able to read? Then read to a child who hasn't mastered this skill yet.

Do you have the ability to smile? Then share your smile with every person you see.

Celebrate and use your abilities! Don't look out your window and give up what you have because you wish you were capable of what someone else is currently doing. Giving Comparison control will deplete your effectiveness in this world and drive you away from your destination. Instead, let's learn to coexist with Comparison and win in this world by staying in control and choosing to use Comparison for good.

Do you currently have control over comparing your achievements with those of others? Rate your level of control on a scale of 1 to 10.

(full control) 1 2 3 4 5 6 7 8 9 10 (no control)

CHAPTER FIVE

Cost Analysis: What is Comparison Costing me?

> **Cost** (n)
> 1. The price paid to acquire, produce, accomplish, or maintain anything
> 2. An expenditure of money, time, labor, trouble, etc.
> 3. A sacrifice, loss, or penalty

Think back on what prompted you to read this book. Perhaps Comparison has been driving your life while you look out the window—are you ready for a change of scenery? Tired of feeling like you're never good enough?

You want to measure up.

You want to win.

You want a solution.

Now that you know how Comparison is affecting your life, you are in the perfect position to use this chapter to help you determine *what* it's costing you.

We will begin learning the WIN Method, beginning with *weighing your cost*.

Cause and Effect.

Without debating causation and correlation, I want you to take a very entry-level look at the idea of cause and effect and how it can help you in your plight to determine your cost and control Comparison in your life. Consider the idea that for every effect there is a cause, and for every cause there is an effect—this gives you tremendous power over Comparison. It means that every thought you have, every action you take, every word you say, every decision you make, has a preceding cause, and it *will* have an impact. Whether the effect created has a positive, negative, or neutral result, there is always an effect. Breaking this down, you'll begin to recognize the power you possess through your actions—it's rather mind-blowing!

For example, the last paragraph I chose to write may cause you to think about your actions through the lens of cause and effect. Say it reminds you of how you spoke harshly to your spouse this morning when you were running late for work and you regrettably realize that those words probably had a negative impact on him, so you choose to take another action. You send an apologetic text message to your husband for your grumpiness, sharing your appreciation for him. That action, which was caused by analyzing your previous cause and effect from reading the paragraph above, now creates a positive impact on your husband's mood.

The effect of his improved outlook causes him to go out of his way to help a coworker with a project, which causes that coworker to leave work on time so he could be at his son's baseball game. The snowball continues to roll down the hill of cause and effect, sometimes with good results, and other times, creating casualties in its path.

How do cause and effect intersect with solving the Comparison epidemic in our lives?

Every comparison we create has a similar effect; it is up to us to figure out *how* it's impacting us and to what extent. More specifically, you must discover and recognize the adverse effect that Comparison is creating in your life.

When we compare, a cause and effect relationship takes place. The adverse effects are the costs we need to analyze as we begin to take control of Comparison in our life.

Weigh the Cost.

The first step in moving forward in any area of your life is to weigh the cost. There's no motivation or reason to fix a problem if you don't know what it's costing you. If it's not costing you anything, there's no problem that needs to be fixed!

Think of a running toilet. Mildly annoyed, you notice the toilet connected to your bedroom is cycling when it shouldn't, and think, *I'll get it fixed eventually*, but you quickly forget. When the noise happens more frequently, and the sudden water cycles wake you up at night, reducing the quality of your sleep, the costs of not fixing the toilet (lack of sleep and irritability) may become high enough to consider taking action.

Say the costs aren't high enough yet. A month into the issue, the water and sewer bills roll in, and you see the financial cost that this running toilet has on your checkbook—you call the plumber immediately! Though you didn't realize it, the problem was costing you money the entire time. If you'd known what it was costing you, you probably would have fixed it sooner and saved money. Now, as with a leaky toilet, ask yourself, *What is Comparison costing me?*

Getting an accurate Comparison cost list can be a rather challenging task for several reasons. For starters, let's come out with it and confess that we don't like admitting to being controlled by Comparison. Being controlled by something has a bad connotation and makes us feel weak. We love to be in control, after all. Most of us notice the detrimental effects of Comparison and long to be free from its hold. However, being completely vulnerable and stating, "Hi, my name is Renee, and I'm a Comparaholic" isn't comfortable.

Admitting to giving Comparison control can give the impression that we are judging other people, or that we're always thinking about ourselves, material stuff, appearances, status, achievements, and so on. I don't want to be perceived as a self-absorbed and judgmental person because that's not who I am—but I *am* a recovering Comparaholic.

Whether or not a recovering alcoholic is thinking about alcohol at the moment, they must acknowledge their problem or tendency, calculate what it costs them, weigh that cost, and then, should they choose to, take the necessary steps to prevent alcohol from controlling their life.

It's similar with Comparison.

We have to realize that the temptation may come at any time. Let go of the perceived stigma and humbly acknowledge Comparison's detrimental potential so you can remove your blinders and see what's really going on around you. How is it wreaking havoc in your life?

No human being alive has perfect control over Comparison, but some of us can identify when

Comparison attempts to take over (and you can be one of them!). Be honest with yourself. Look Comparison in the eye and see how it's stealing your time, ruining your relationships, stripping you of opportunities, costing you money and who knows what else.

We also need to assess and calculate the cost because Comparison has the tendency to be subtle—so subtle that we fail to recognize it for what it is and mistake it for something else. Our human minds typically try to displace blame wherever possible, which can keep us from going deep enough to figure out when Comparison may be at work. Stopping short, we cast blame on outside elements, like other people's successes or failures, our lack of resources, unfortunate circumstances—even the weather—yet we fail to see how we are giving Comparison control and allowing it to hide behind other excuses. Why do we do this? Because it's easier to place fault on something outside of our control than it is to work on internal issues that we *could* have control over, but don't.

In my mid-twenties, I was blessed to be able to stay home with our two young kids, and yet I always felt the nagging urge to do more. I decided to be a distributor for a direct sales company and sell nutritional products that I liked. Helping people find health results like my family had experienced gave me a sense of added purpose and the idea of earning extra income inspired me to work harder in hopes that my husband wouldn't have to be gone working so much. I was on a mission.

In an attempt to learn how to grow my business, I focused on successful people in the company spotlight. Watching them replace incomes and live the dream, I became very unsettled with my own status. The moms I met at conferences made it seem so easy, so I kept pushing myself. I wanted what they had—financial and family freedom—and I was determined to achieve it.

Though I put in the hours, I still wasn't earning enough income to achieve the goal I was after, namely, "bring my husband home." During the day, I began to feel resentful and exasperated toward my children when their naps didn't go as planned, and my business calls were disrupted. I stayed up late on the phone during the evenings, which didn't thrill my husband. Thus, I became bitter toward him for not supporting me.

Looking back to calculate the cost of Comparison, I see some pretty big expenditures my family had to endure as I pursued the success that others in the company were having. Not only did I fail to appreciate my time with my little kiddos as much as I could, but my focus wasn't in the right place regarding my marriage, either. The irony is that I was doing all of this to have more quality family time!

There are plenty of scapegoat options I could choose to blame for the stress that my family and I were experiencing without the desired payout. Some blame the industry as a whole, saying that direct sales and multi-level marketing opportunities offer big promises with little payoff. People from other direct sales companies blame the company, claiming the business system must not work. Those within the company may think I failed to follow their system correctly. It would be easy to claim that I wasn't cut out for the business, or it wasn't the right timing. Whether any shred of truth exists in any of those theories, a huge reason for the stress is this: I gave Comparison control. To see this, I had to retrace my thoughts and allow my mind to go deeper.

When you dig deep to reveal the costs of Comparison, you'll find it is kind of like peeling an onion. At first glance, the onion is a harmless round object with a dull brown layer on the outside. There's nothing significant about it. Taking off the first layer, you notice it looks a bit different beneath the surface, but still isn't a threat. When you take off another layer, a pungent smell fills the air that wasn't noticeable before. By the third layer, the juicy white flesh and its tear-inducing fumes are very apparent. Your eyes burn, and tears form. The detrimental effects of a Comparison-controlled life are often found deep beneath the surface.

How can you peel the onion of your mind to reveal the stinky parts about what Comparison is costing you? I use a method that I call the Deeper Question Approach, which is when we question a statement by asking *who, what, where, when, why,* or *how* to every answer to go deeper and get to the bottom of any issue. It works best when someone else is asking the questions, but you can practice on your own as well. Though it can go in many different directions, it usually helps to uncover hidden costs that we didn't realize were affecting us.

Here's a possible rendition for the situation I just shared:

Why was I experiencing relational stress?
I felt like my kids and my husband were keeping me from reaching my goals.

What were my goals?
To make enough money so that my husband could work less and be home more.

Why did I want my husband to be home more?
So, we could enjoy more family time, and I could get some time to myself.

What made me want to have more family time and time to myself—what would it look like?

I felt like we were missing out on what we could have. Many husbands spend time with the family on evenings and weekends. It would be nice to go out for date night every once in a while. I also wanted to get out of the house more (without kids) and attend some evening events with friends. I wanted less stress and more fun. Seeing families on TV or real families on social media reminded me of the warm happy family feeling I was missing out on.

As a young wife and mom observing other families enjoying their nights and weekends together, I gave Comparison the wheel. I also succumbed to handing over control when I saw other friends together having fun without kids in tow, and I felt left out.

Though I wanted what I didn't have, I needed to choose to appreciate what I did have. Lack of gratitude is a critical component in recognizing Comparison's control.

I compared my lack of success to moms with successful direct-sales businesses working for them. *If they were making six figures, what was I doing wrong?* I was dedicated, friendly, smart, and I had a college degree. These were all good things, so what was I missing?

I mentioned previously how some people tend to shut down when they're face to face with Comparison, but that's not me. I'm naturally competitive. I pushed harder and worked longer. Meanwhile, I became more frustrated and blamed others when I didn't measure up to whatever I was measuring myself to. When I think about it now, I see that giving Comparison control cost me precious time with my little ones as well as contentment. Then there's the financial cost of money

I spent on resources and events I attended because top company performers told me these things would help to reach my goals, and I wanted to be like them. One recommended trip to Staples cost me $40 for a silly planner that I never actually used. Who knows how much further I could break it down and how much more it truly cost me?

Before you start thinking I'm making Comparison out to be the reason for the fall of humankind (oh, wait, I already did that in Chapter One), let's keep in mind that we are multifaceted people with complex problems requiring a conglomeration of solutions—but we have to start somewhere. Taking control over Comparison and weighing our cost is a great starting place, but other factors may be present as well. Knowing that Comparison may only be a part of the overall equation can further challenge calculating the actual cost of Comparison.

My friend Taylor deals with a social anxiety disorder. She rarely leaves her house other than going to work and the occasional trip to the store. The thought of making new friends, going to church or a gym, or doing anything in public settings overwhelms her. In addition to anxiety, she deals with weight issues, low self-esteem, and procrastination and constantly compares herself to others regarding these issues. Part of her anxiety for going to the gym or meeting new people is that she won't know what to do or say. She stresses over what people will think about her. Which came first: the social anxiety disorder or obsessing over what others think? Perhaps she's predisposed to the anxiety disorder and trauma triggered it—who knows?

It doesn't really matter. Most likely, there's a dual causality relationship between Taylor's anxiety disorder and her giving Comparison control. We could easily blame the anxiety disorder and call Comparison a symptom, but why not calculate the costs of Comparison having control and see how it might influence her anxiety disorder? Maybe it could reduce the adverse thought patterns that fuel the cycle.

For Taylor, the Deep Question Approach could look something like this:

Why do I get so anxious about being around people?
Because they'll probably think I'm fat and stupid.

What makes me think they will think that I'm fat and stupid?
Because I'm overweight and everyone looks better than me, so I get nervous. I can't think of what to say, so I say stupid things, or I don't talk at all and look dumb.

Why do I care if others look better than me?
Because everyone thinks to look good, you have to be skinny, and I'm not. So, I don't fit in.

Who has said I don't fit in?
I guess no one in particular, but that's because I don't put myself in the position for people to talk to me much.

What's the worst that could happen if I put myself in a position for people to get to know me?
They'll judge me.

What would happen if I were judged?
I'd feel bad.

Don't I already feel bad about not going out and doing things, meeting people, or getting exercise?
Yes.

So, I feel bad regardless of whether I go out and feel anxious, or I stay home to not feel anxious?
Yeah, pretty much. My life is a mess.

Why don't I take small steps toward getting out and exercising so that I can feel better about myself?
Because it takes work. Wow, that's convicting—I sound really lazy.

What would be a good first step I can take, and when will I execute it?
I should develop a plan.

For Taylor, comparing her weight to others' is currently costing her relationships, stress, and opportunities. It's also keeping her from improving her health and potentially improving her mental health. It's definitely keeping her from seeing any success. If Taylor could overcome the worry of what others will think of her and devises a plan to get out and begin exercising, she could learn a lot from the confidence of experiencing success, even if it's a slow, steady process. Statistically, she'll also reduce anxiety and improve her overall health, according to many studies conducted regarding the relationship between exercise and anxiety.

It's worth noting that Comparison can trigger effects (aka costs) that are potentially life-threatening and need professional attention—beyond dealing with Comparison itself. A notable example of this was brought to us by the late Princess of Wales, Princess Diana. She publicly shared her struggle with bulimia in a 1992 private interview with BBC,[21] bringing the necessary mental health component to the surface versus the thought of merely wanting to be thin. Comparison can factor into the equation, however, as a triggering element. Since that time, researchers have learned that individuals may be predisposed to specific mental health conditions, such as bulimia, which may remain dormant until something triggers it. Diana recounted Prince Charles making a comment about her "getting rather chubby," when they were on their honeymoon, which began her spiral.[22] Not measuring up to another's expectations—even if they're perceived expectations—is a common reason that people allow Comparison to take over. This is an excellent reminder to be mindful of our own words and our expectations of others.

When Comparison is intermingled with another issue or disguised by a similar attribute to itself, the two may seem undifferentiated, making it difficult to calculate the costs of Comparison. Characteristics such as competition or ambition can begin innocently and then quickly morph. Though we start with pure motives, Comparison often hijacks the scene wearing the mask of something that society says is okay, like competition. Anytime Comparison takes charge, the costs are high and accrue the same problems. Remember how the lines blurred for Lance Armstrong between competing to be the best athlete and taking a negative detour when Comparison took the wheel. To uncover some of the deep-rooted costs, we must be authentic and willing to let go of our conscious and unconscious motives to see the reality of what is currently taking place.

Now that we've addressed some of the potential obstacles that get in the way of calculating the expenses related to Comparison, you should be prepared to move forward with the first step of measuring up and winning: creating a detailed cost analysis of your own life so you can weigh the cost of allowing Comparison to take over your journey. Start your engines, here we go!

Conducting a Comparison Cost Analysis.

For those who want to have control over Comparison, developing this Comparison Cost Analysis is the vital first step. It provides the fuel and motivation you'll need later to measure up to your Innovated Identity and Navigate your Journey to win.

Just as a successful business conducts a routine cost analysis to identify where they can reduce costs and run their business more effectively, you will perform a cost analysis of Comparison in your life. Then you will develop a plan to ultimately help you claim control and live your life with more intention. Who wants to be paying for something that's actually harmful? Not to mention, it's dangerous to give up control of something as valuable as your mind to any other entity, including Comparison.

Begin by identifying some of the roads and destinations you travel in your life journey. The roads you travel could be the roles or labels you apply to yourself. The destinations are the goals or dreams you pursue within each of those roles.

Some potential roads/roles you may be driving on:

Friend	Volunteer
Spouse	Neighbor
Entrepreneur	Parent
Employer	Single Person
Employee	Daughter
Student	Other _____

How does Comparison attempt to sneak control over your mind in each of your roles, and what does it cost you when it succeeds?

Think back to some of the previous examples.

Though there's not always a negative outcome, anything can provide an opportunity for comparing yourself (or others) against something or someone. You may even compare yourself to the expectations you have for yourself in a particular role. For example, as a wife, perhaps you expect yourself to cook dinner every weeknight and then compare yourself to other wives who do it better (or don't cook at all).

The same goes for your destinations and goals. We often measure our progress for achieving our goals to someone else's results. Sometimes we compare our expectations of where we should be on a particular road to someone else's location.

These are some potential destinations/goals you may be heading toward:

Earning a Degree	A Promotion
Having Children	Finding a Spouse
Owning a Home	Being an Industry Leader
Owning Business	Other_____
Becoming Profitable	

To get your mental gears turning for your personal Comparison Cost Analysis, I've provided you with some examples. Take a look at the Comparison Cost Analysis Table on page 90. Note the three Comparison Roadblocks at the top and some potential costs listed in the left-hand column to stimulate thinking. Specific actions that happen when Comparison is driving are where they intersect. For instance, take a peek under *Assets*. When Comparison controls your thinking, you might long for a nicer home, and though you aren't in the market to purchase right now, this desire causes you to spend numerous hours scrolling through homes for sale in your area. This Comparison-controlled thought may not cost you money, but what does it cost you?

Time.

You can more accurately calculate the time wasted by using an app to track the hours per week you spend on the MLS website, or wherever you're spending your limited time. Check out additional costs associated with activities that can occur when Comparison Roadblocks get between us and our destination:

Comparison Cost Analysis Table

Costs	Assets	Appearances	Achievements
Time	Researching new houses	Shopping for cosmetics/hair/ skincare/etc.	Working after hours on a project to get ahead
Money	Living in a neigh- borhood where it's challenging to afford to keep up with the lifestyle	Having teeth whitening, high- lights, manicures, pedicures, Botox, tanning	Obtaining certi- fications, degrees, higher education
Opportunities	Refusing financial help because you don't want others to see you're not as well off as they are	Refusing to enjoy a beach vacation because you don't feel you look good in a swimsuit	Avoiding entering a contest when you see other excellent candidates
Relationships	Avoiding enter- taining guests because you're embarrassed by your home	Missing out on a potential friend- ship because you feel inferior to her attractiveness	Deciding a coworker is a rival
Confidence	Thinking someone else is better than you because they have more money or material items	Refraining from a fashion you love because you think you won't look as good as others in it	Feeling shame for not winning first place
Health	Carrying the heavy designer purse that hurts your neck and shoulders	Wearing attractive high heels despite the pain and blisters they cause	Getting inade- quate sleep due to overworking
Spiritual	Valuing people according to their possessions or lifestyle	Concluding that God made a mistake when He created your body	Believing you must earn approval from God
Freedom	Being enslaved to unnecessary debt	Refusing to be seen unless makeup and hair look good	Imposing rigid accomplishment guidelines on yourself
Reputation	Attempting to keep up or outdo others repulses people; could cause a reputation of arrogance	Attempting to impress others with your looks, leading to the reputation of self-consumption or not relatable	Earning a reputa- tion for the need to be the best in whatever you participate
Other...			

This is far from an exhaustive list of costs and only scratches the surface of those associated with Comparison. Dig deeper to expose what Comparison is costing you. Start by determining your cause and effect relationships with each of the Comparison roadblocks and note your discoveries. Look for current examples as well as those that have cost you in the past. Contemplate the roles you perform and the associated goals to reach your destination—there could be hidden costs. Identify any costs that accrue when Comparison even hints at being in control. Be as specific as possible. For example, how much time per month do you spend engaging in appearance-based activities that you wouldn't if Comparison weren't involved? Don't be shy; include travel time and gas expense for those trips to the salon. In addition to the actual cost of each item bought, how much interest are you accruing each month due to credit card debt for purchases you really didn't need?

Additional costs may surface when looking beyond the immediate impact and examining how they could affect your future as well.

For example, if you get in debt to measure up in the Assets department, how could this affect your future financial situation? Maybe it will impede you from obtaining a better credit score, reducing your chances of owning a home later. Current debt could result in a higher interest rate when applying for a loan or affect your ability get a loan at all. Keeping up with the Joneses might be preventing you from paying off your student loans, building an emergency fund, or preparing for retirement. If so, envision how your future may look different.

Maybe it's time to ask yourself if you really need that new car that comes with a higher payment, the manicure every few weeks, another tattoo, or a new dress to wear to that party? Will anyone remember, or care, if you wear one you've worn before? Is it worth the overall cost?

How about your health? If you're not getting the sleep that your body so desperately needs because Comparison drives your achievements, then a little research will show you what your sleep deficit is doing to your long-term health and happiness. Do you want to rob your future by allowing Comparison to splurge on your present?

> Do you want to rob your future by allowing Comparison to splurge on your present?

Typically, the costs resulting from your Comparison-controlled living affect more than yourself; they also negatively impact others.

If you are racking up debt now and are raising children (or plan to in the future), think about the significant impact it could have on your family—the neighborhood you can afford to live in, their school district, and perhaps where they go to college.

If you are married or plan to be at some point, have you thought about retirement and your future plans together? Maybe you'd like to travel together someday. What you choose to spend your assets on now has a direct effect on whether you'll be able to afford to retire or travel. Taking care of your health today affects what you can do down the road. Will you be able to travel to see your grandchildren and spoil them like crazy? Forgive my morbidity but think of the burden you might leave for others to deal with when you pass away with a heap of debt or a houseful of junk—in part because you continue to let Comparison drive your life. Is it worth it?

Early on in my coaching business, I stared at coaches who had accreditations and certifications—as well as confidence—that I didn't yet have. When Comparison controlled my mind, the story I told myself was that I wasn't as good as other coaches, so I didn't promote myself. Comparing my lack of achievements to others' cost me potential influence and income. I lost growth and impact that could've been taking place had I not sabotaged the opportunities to work with them. Allowing Comparison to drive my life meant that I was robbing potential from others with whom I could have been working by stifling my gifts—because I focused on others' abilities and achievements instead of my own. After weighing the cost, I discovered it wasn't worth it.

Since we can't track every Comparison-controlled thought or action, we'll never figure out the entire Comparison Cost Analysis and expenses that accrue (but we can do our best).

Where are you with this? What have you learned about yourself and the cost of Comparison in your life? Are there areas in which you need to spend a little more time peeling back layers to reveal what's underneath? Whether you've identified many areas or only a few affected by Comparison, calculate the cost you've already paid, what it potentially will cost, and what that means for your life and the life of others.

Once you identify and calculate what you're spending due to Comparison's control, you'll inevitably develop a deeper desire to eliminate these costs and reclaim your driver seat. Imagine your life as you sit confidently driving toward your destination.

You may live in a world that wants to keep you on the bandwagon of Comparaholics, but now is the time to learn how to jump off.

Considering the costs that you're incurring, how expensive is Comparison in your life on a scale of 1 to 10?

(cheap) 1 2 3 4 5 6 7 8 9 10 (expensive)

PART 2
INNOVATE YOUR IDENTITY

CHAPTER SIX
Identity Crisis: Who am I?

Identity Crisis (n)
A period of uncertainty and confusion in which a person's sense of identity becomes insecure, typically due to a change in their expected aims or role in society.

Have you ever had an identity crisis? Perhaps you're experiencing one right now and don't even realize it. How can you find out? Read on to learn.

My educational background is in psychology. It's an easy decision for me to seek out counseling when areas in my life are due for improvement. Similar to stopping for directions when I'm lost or when I want to make sure I'm on the right path—there's no shame. Sometimes I'll even go for a regular tune-up to ensure proper maintenance.

Several years ago, I realized my check engine light had come on and scheduled an appointment. The counselor was a spunky lady in her 70s with exponential wisdom and insight. It became clear I needed to do some major identity work and figure out who the real Renee Vidor was—she was the right person to help me. She repeated a statement over and over that I simply couldn't grasp:

"Renee, you're exhausted. You've got to stop performing."

It annoyed me.

"Yeah, I'm exhausted, alright. I'm parenting two active kids and a dog, I'm a wife, and I maintain a household. I'm a school room parent and a business partner, and I'm active in my church and the local community. I plan events and volunteer, and try to keep up with many great friends—but performing? That's not me."

I equated performing with being phony or living out a drama queen persona, however, she wasn't referring to drama and it had nothing to do with me being a fake. It took a long time for me to comprehend that she actually meant I was turning to people-pleasing and working for approval. Once I understood, it took even longer to realize how to stop this performing. I was constantly trying to measure up and was in a continual state of Comparison without even realizing it.

I was suffering from an identity crisis. That realization was the beginning of a journey that has ultimately led me to clarity and freedom that I didn't realize could exist.

Now I look back and see myself as a performer on the stage called life. I acted out scripts for every role that I had: wife, mother, entrepreneur, friend and so on. If I failed to play my part perfectly, or I didn't earn the intended applause or response from the audience, then I felt like I didn't measure up to the standards for that role. When I thought I wasn't measuring up, I felt as if I was letting people down. It was crushing—I wasn't enough. I didn't have a safe place to get away from all of the roles because I had locked my identity in them.

When I first realized I was playing to these scripts, I felt enslaved by them, like they were shackles around my wrist. I became angry. Blame often follows anger, and my first reaction was to blame the people I thought were writing these scripts for me.

I blamed those perfect mothers who made my imperfections stand out. The volunteers who had what I thought was "all the time in the world" to help and made me seem lazy drove me crazy. Then there's our society that expected me to be flawless and put together whenever I stepped out of the house, putting so much pressure on me!

I felt some resentment toward friends who thought I should be available whenever they called, and even toward my husband who had unmet expectations of me yet didn't see or appreciate all I was doing. Putting in hours upon hours of practice trying to memorize and act out all my parts the right way for everyone left me feeling exhausted.

Despite all of this, I still didn't feel like I measured up. There was always more I could and should be doing better. I relentlessly tried to measure up to other's standards.

Soon came the next stage of awareness: were these playwrights actually putting expectations on me and writing these scripts? Nope.

The screenwriter, director, and producer of the *Measuring Up with Renee* show was none other than . . . me.

If any of the individuals previously mentioned had contributed to the scripts I was writing for my life, it was because I had given them permission and power to do so. I had given up the rights to my identity.

It was *me* trying to measure up to *my* expectations that I had developed for myself due to what I perceived others wanted or expected of me.

Many of these expectations were false and self-imposed. Some were authored from a mere fraction of truth and blown out of proportion. Nonetheless, comparing myself to them left me feeling like I was never enough.

Once I realized everything I had been using to create my identity wasn't my identity at all, I felt unsettled. I was going through an identity crisis. Who was I?

The perceived identity that I had been putting so much effort into was actually a fake ID.

Sure, I could easily use it to get by in many aspects of my life—like business meetings or social gatherings. It was pretty easy to be the person I was performing to be—she wasn't a bad person—but like any other fake ID, when it came down to the real deal, it wasn't cutting it. When I wanted to travel across the country border to drive forward into new territory, my fake identity was rejected. I wasn't able to access the next step of personal growth until something changed.

Thankfully, my counselor called me out: I needed an authentic, valid ID to process through the security and get to the next leg of my life journey. Ignorance was no longer bliss; now that I was aware, I couldn't pass through life with a fake ID anymore.

Measuring Up.

This entire process started with an internal voice that kept telling me, "You're not measuring up, Renee."

We frequently use the phrase *measure up* in our everyday vernacular, but it wasn't until researching for this book that I learned that the verbs *perform* and *carry out* are linked to this common phrase. Sound familiar? *To measure up* can mean "reaching a certain standard" or "to be capable" or "qualified; to be equal, high enough quality."

As much as I tried, I didn't feel qualified, equal to others, or like I met the quality status quo. I was performing in an attempt to reach fictitious standards I had imposed upon myself—as a business owner, as a mom, as a wife, as a woman. I would compare myself to that moving target, and to anyone else I thought had attained it, but always felt defeated because I could never score a bull's eye in any aspect of my life. I wasn't measuring up.

Where do these standards and images in our fake identities come from in the first place?

Sometimes they are linked to those three Comparison roadblocks: *Assets*, *Appearance*, and *Achievement*. In my own personal processing, this is what I found:

Assets: We were living in a suburb that is known for luxurious living. We owned a beautiful home we built, and we had more than I'd ever dreamed of. However, I often felt like my house, my minivan, and my neighborhood didn't measure up in the minds of other moms from my children's school. I lived on the outskirts of the million dollar home neighborhoods. As a naturally practical person unmotivated by materialism, I didn't desire expensive jewelry or spend on designer clothing (unless they were treasures unburied at the local thrift store). My lifestyle didn't reflect that of others. Getting manicures, pedicures, massages, and regular luncheon and Starbucks® splurges weren't my jive—whether or not others actually noticed I was different, I did.

Appearance: I focused on the difference between myself and models, women portrayed in the media, and Hollywood celebrities. Looking at local ladies in my area, I didn't have the beautiful straight hair they did, and my makeup was basic. As a redhead with a fair complexion, I was never going to have the beautiful summer tan everyone else rocked. I felt unpretty when I compared myself to other women. When I thought about my very handsome husband, I wondered how he got stuck with *me*? I didn't think I measured up to what he could have married and believed he could've been happier waking up to see someone else day after day.

Achievement: Having our first child at the age of 21, I was younger than the average mom in my area. Living in a mostly two-income, career-focused area, the majority of my children's peers' parents were upwards of a decade older than me with important titles and careers. Sometimes I felt like I didn't measure up or wasn't as well-received because of my youth and lack of status as a stay-at-home mom—despite having a college degree and entrepreneurial spirit.

Comparison held the keys to my life which was causing me to live with a fake ID.

It's Not Entirely Our Fault.

When I was a kid, I remember being intrigued by my parents' driver's licenses and wanting so badly to have one of my own. Not only did it permit them to drive, but something about the official looking plastic card made it a status icon in my mind signifying importance and validation.

My friends and I would create versions for ourselves by cutting rectangles out of cereal boxes and drawing our pictures in the corner. While we didn't know what they meant, we would transcribe the numbers and symbols from the genuine license, trying to replicate the authentic one. Then we'd proudly ride our bikes around the neighborhood pretending we were adults with our "driver's license."

As children, we role-play. We called it playing pretend. Imaginative play is an essential part of childhood development and is how we practice and learn to experience life for ourselves. However, unbeknownst to us, our role-playing can trickle into our later years and cause problems. Role-playing is when we pretend to be someone or something else. As a child, it could be anything—a puppy, a teacher, a Disney princess (or even a real driver with a valid license). As we mature, society provides parameters around what it deems appropriate, or what it wants us to be. For instance, it's favorable to be a doctor or lawyer for money and status. We fix our eyes on titles, roles, and desires that can implant in us a desire for an identity that isn't genuinely ours.

Well-meaning adults ask the question all throughout a child's life. *What do you want to be when you grow up?* It's readily answered with job titles such as veterinarian, singer, teacher, engineer, dentist, author, and so forth.

From an early age, we unintentionally confuse our identity with our profession, and this confusion carries on into adulthood. These job titles are merely skill sets we learn to perform in order to pay our bills and fill our time; they are what we *do*—not who we *are*. How might the mindsets of future generations change if we rephrase the question to something like, *What interests you?*

If we groom our youth to believe that their occupation is the root of their importance, then we pave the way for them to be stuck in an identity crisis. By teaching *what we do* is *who we are*, we equate an individual's worth and value with a position, job, or role—any of which could disappear in an instant. If those things do cease to exist or never come to fruition in the first place, then who are we? When we lose our ability to work due to an injury or our job is downsized or we are struggling with infertility, and the dream of the mom title is lost—are we then worthless?

Our identity is more than our social status or our ability to create income. There has to be something more to look forward to than being an occupation or a role.

What is Your Current ID?

I already shared what my identity looked like several years ago. It was a fake comprised of what I *had* and what I *did*—aka my acquisitions and roles. "I *have* two children (I'm a mom), I *have* a husband (I'm a wife), I *have* a dog (I'm a pet owner), I *have* a household to maintain (I clean, cook, grocery shop and more)." Blah, blah, blah.

While my acquisitions—my children, husband, dog, and house—are important to me, and the roles are also meaningful, it didn't serve me well to continue carrying those around as a fake ID. They are part of me, but they aren't who I *am*.

What if my husband were to walk out on me or pass away? What happens when my children go off to college, when my dog dies, if my house burns down, or my business fails, and we run out of money? It sounds like a country song, but any of it can be real life. What if it becomes illegal to go to church or my friends disown me, or if I no longer have time to volunteer? Who am I then?

What about you? What is your current identity? Is it a fake one, relying on your roles and acquisitions? My guess is yes, because most are.

Reverse and the Rearview Mirror.

Not all facets of our fake ID are derived from the current comparisons we make. Some aspects come from our past. We've all been called names and have been assigned adjectives by others, dating as far back as childhood.

Smart, pretty, rebellious, stupid, sassy, quiet, or loud. Labels come in all shapes and sizes, and once tagged, they often adhere and embed themselves into your fake ID. They may even trigger an identity crisis.

When labels stick to us, they create an invitation for Comparison to enter our vehicle and take control—including positive labels. People are well meaning and will often tell you good things you like to hear (i.e., you're attractive, you look like a model, you're so skinny, you're very smart, you're the best volleyball player on the team). Still, even when accurate, those compliments are not who you are as a person, and you shouldn't rely on them for your identity. Positive labels stuck on us are difficult to measure up to and require effort to maintain. Most cannot be sustained over time, so we feel like we don't measure up.

Negative labels pose an opposite but equally detrimental problem. Were you the class clown who often got into trouble, or maybe you were called dumb for being held back a year in school? These labels are not who you are, and you don't have to measure up to what they claim, nor do they need to be part of your identity.

Even neutral labels can hinder us in discovering our true identity. Were you a sassy child? Maybe you tended to be loud and rambunctious, or were on the shy side. These and other labeled attributes can pose a problem in your present and future life if they're mistaken for being your identity.

A person can speak a simple characteristic into existence, and we claim it as our identity, feeling compelled to exhibit it because it's what we know—but we don't have to! Never give another human being the power to dictate your identity.

> Never give another human being the power to dictate your identity.

Maybe you're thinking, *I've given myself labels due to what I've done or what others have done to me in my past.* Don't permit your past to dictate your future—or your identity.

The highly esteemed and successful Oprah Winfrey was sexually abused by family members beginning at the age of nine years old. At age 14, she became pregnant from one of the sexual encounters. The baby was born prematurely and died weeks later, leaving Oprah to hold the pain, disgrace, and shame inside for many years.[23] In the February 2007 issue of *O, The Oprah Magazine,* she wrote, "I imagined that every person on the street was going to point their finger at me and scream, 'Pregnant at 14, you wicked girl. . . .'"The label of wicked girl was part of her fake identity until a family member leaked her story many years later. That breach released Oprah to deal with the heavy burden she had been hiding inside, leading her toward freedom from the label and closer to her true identity.

Though our experiences do, in fact, play a role in defining who we become, dwelling on the rearview mirror is dangerous. It's meant for glancing. In other words, you may need to use it to maneuver backward into a tight parking spot, or to back out of your garage, but if you continue to stare in the rearview mirror while driving forward, you're guaranteed to crash.

The same goes for driving in reverse. Our lives, like cars, are meant to be experienced by moving forward. We live in the present and plan for the future. There is a time and a place to revisit our past, but no one gets ahead by driving in reverse. We may have to back up a few feet to reposition for our future, but those moments shouldn't be our primary methods of operating our vehicles—or our lives.

Unfortunately, some people in your life may not want you to drive forward. Instead, they'll continually remind you of your past, telling you it dictates your identity and your future. Perhaps they don't want you to get ahead of them in their life journey, so as you start to move forward toward your destination, they drive behind you, shining their bright lights to blind and distract you. They don't want you to grow, so they try to get you to pull over by reminding you of your fake ID.

Instead of looking in the rearview mirror or pulling over for unnecessary stops, flip that mirror up to the night position to avoid being blinded, focus on the journey ahead by keeping your foot on the gas, and drive forward toward discovering your authentic and valid identity.

Lost or Stolen ID.

To operate a motor vehicle legally, we are required to possess a valid driver's license, which also serves as our legal identification, or ID. Whether we drive or not, adults are required to have some form of official government identification for proving who we are when we do things like apply for a job, an apartment, or travel by airplane.

If you lose your ID or don't own one, you are limited in what you can do or accomplish. You have to figure out how to live life on the outskirts, trying to make ends meet without getting in trouble with the law.

When I was in high school, I worked at a local family-owned Mexican restaurant. Not all employees were legal US citizens, including a 15-year-old boy named Pedro. Pedro hadn't been in school for years because he lacked the proper identification. Though only a couple of years older than Pedro, I saw the importance of education and advocated for him to obtain the necessary credentials to begin attending high school. While it's possible to live and function in our society without proper ID, restrictions may keep us from taking advantage of great opportunities. Without a valid ID, Pedro didn't have access to education, and other things that would help him find and live out his potential—the same is true for us, figuratively speaking.

Sometimes we've obtained our ID, but we lose it, or someone steals it from us. My parents were able to join our family on a recent trip to Italy. We were all enjoying touring Rome when my dad made the gut-wrenching realization that his passport and driver's license were no longer in his pocket. He had to go through an exceptionally prolonged process at the embassy (and pay a fee) to obtain new valid identification. Without those critical documents, he wasn't going to be able to leave Italy to get back home.

Similarly, discovering our identity is essential for us to reach our destination as it keeps us from giving Comparison control of our lives. Many of us don't have it in our possession. It may have gotten lost along your rocky life journey, or perhaps it was misplaced when you entered motherhood. A ruthless boss or a former abuser may have stolen it from you, or perhaps you never knew your identity in the first place.

Though we don't get in legal trouble for not possessing our true identity, the negative impact and ramifications are endless. Just as it's hard to get to your destination with a fake ID, you are more likely to hand Comparison the wheel when you're insecure and don't know who you are. Living with an ambiguous identity is a roadmap to disaster as social standards yell at us to measure up to *this* kind of person and shame us for not being as good as *that* person. Billboards offer a picture to imitate, bosses give an outline to conform to, spouses share a list of ways to improve; meanwhile, we feel confused, frustrated, and deflated. All of this information conflicts with each other, as well as with how we personally feel. *Who am I supposed to be?*

Recognizing when we are in an identity crisis is essential to measuring up and winning. Whether you've been trying to live out the wrong identity through our fake ID, your identity has been lost or stolen from through hard circumstances or abusive people, or you've been living in hiding like an illegal citizen—if you don't have it already, *now* is the time to start the process to obtain your valid license for your life—your *real* identity.

I'm here to walk beside you; I've been there. I had a fake ID that looked fairly good from the outside. However, it was an identity that had been manipulated by abusers in my past, hurt by friends who betrayed me, and became confused and lost when I took on the roles of wife and mother. We were not created to live our lives in the state of confusion. My identity needed to be innovated, and I'm so grateful that I did it!

I didn't win in a blink of an eye. I followed the steps and stayed the course. My counselor was an excellent guide, as were a few others along the way, but much of the effort was for me to put in on my own. The freedom that has come from innovating my identity was totally worth the effort, and now I'm driving toward my destination without Comparison stealing my wheel.

In the next couple of chapters, you'll learn more about the Innovated Identity and how to *Innovate Your Identity*. You will work through the identity crisis so you can turn in your fake ID and exchange it for your Innovated Identity. It will become what you measure up to, and how you will win as you claim control over Comparison. Comparison doesn't have a chance to steal the wheel when a woman is measuring up to her Innovated Identity!

On a scale of 1 to 10, where would you say you are on the continuum of identity crisis?

(Perfect ID) 1 2 3 4 5 6 7 8 9 10 (lost, stolen, or fake ID)

CHAPTER SEVEN

The Perfect Life:
"Who do I want to be?"

> **Innovate** (v)
> Make changes in something established, especially by
> introducing new methods, ideas, or products.

How often do you catch yourself looking out your window, comparing yourself to others, trying to measure up to the world's standards? The longer we stare, the higher the likelihood that the world's standards become our own belief system. We begin to think that someone else's life is supposed to be our reality. What we believe and measure ourselves against affects *who* we are.

What would it look like if we took a fraction of the time we spent comparing ourselves and invested it into *improving* our self and innovating our identity? If every person chose to invest time in learning how to claim control over Comparison instead of spending hours of scrolling through Instagram, Facebook, and the latest Pottery Barn catalogue, drooling over all the things we wish we had, we'd be living in a different world! Instead of a world of Comparison, it would be a world of Confidence—people being who they were created to be and doing what they were designed to do. How freeing would that be? No more feeling inadequate or refraining from action because fear keeps us from stepping out.

For now, we're still living in a world of Comparison, and I applaud you for the time you're investing to improve right now! Let's get to work and learn how to develop your Innovated Identity. It will be your key to measuring up and staying in control over Comparison.

So, what exactly is an Innovated Identity?

Your Innovated Identity is the updated identity you get when you assess the makings of your current identity, remove what doesn't belong, and add in what should be there. It's a personalized template to help you measure up to the person that *you* were created to be—your Innovated Identity!

You must innovate your own identity—no one can do it for you. It would be so much easier if someone could psychoanalyze you and say, "Here you go; I've innovated your identity for you. Now go measure up to it!" We were designed to improve through struggle. I think there's a reason the time machine doesn't exist: God knows we'd miss out on the lessons we grow through and the beauty we experience on the journey along the road trips of life. Identity is no different. You must work on your current identity, customizing and updating it, configuring it closer to the *you* that you were created to be. Once your Innovated Identity is established, it will be a benchmark to help you see what you want to be;

no more trying to be like someone else or measuring up to unrealistic or ambiguous standards.

Though not instantaneously, you can morph into that innovated version of you. If you've identified your Comparison roadblocks and completed your Comparison Cost Analysis, you've paved the way to create your Innovated Identity.

Of course you are *you*, but you're not yet the final version of yourself. Regardless of where you are in this identity process, you have the opportunity to innovate your identity. You can't authentically become someone you weren't created to be—you wouldn't like that person anyhow—but by exploring who you wish you could become, you'll discover deep-rooted desires within that will help you uncover more about the real you that was born to shine.

Self-Exploration.

Innovation begins with self-exploration. Some questions you may ask yourself to help you get started might be:

- What do you look like in your own eyes? Through another's eyes?
- What do you love about yourself? Dislike about yourself?
- Looking back, what are some things that you really wanted to achieve, to be, or to have?
- Are any of those desires still current? Which ones did you achieve?
- Of the ones that never came to fruition, and you have no further desire for them, why do you think they went away?
- Are there any common links that might still be present?

For instance, imagine you wanted to be a teacher when you were a child, but now the very idea of it makes you cringe. Perhaps there is something about teaching others a new skill, or helping people have those light bulb moments that still intrigues you. You may not be created to be a teacher, but perhaps there's an element of teaching that is part of your Innovated Identity—it just looks different than it once did.

During my personal self-exploration, I recalled an instance of something I was passionate about when I was a young teen. I did eventually achieve it, and the process of doing so reminded me of the process of innovating my identity, so I'll share it with you.

Like most teens, I wanted to become a legal driver. To achieve this, I had to follow an official process to obtain a valid driver's license. I began by studying a booklet to learn the facts I needed to know, so the day I turned 15 ½ I could go to the Bureau of Motor Vehicles (BMV) and take a 40 question test in hopes of getting my learner's permit. When I passed that test, in exchange for regurgitating my head knowledge, I was awarded a plastic card with my picture on it. This *learner's permit* gave me the privilege of legally driving on public roads.

Though it was a necessary step toward my eventual freedom, it wasn't my final destination, and it came with restrictions. For the restrictions to be lifted, I had to be 16 years old, complete many hours of supervised driving, and then pass the driver's test.

Leaving the BMV the day I got my learner's permit, my mom allowed me to drive the car home on the streets for the first time to begin my supervised driving hours (I hope I can be as brave as my mom was, when my son begins this journey in less than a year!)

The twenty-minute drive home felt like forever behind the wheel of the family station wagon for the first time. I saw everything from an unfamiliar perspective. Sitting in the driver's seat, I noticed that cars were coming at me quickly, only a few feet away in the next lane. Glancing in the rearview mirror at my younger siblings in the backseat, it hit me: driving a car was a tremendous responsibility! Obtaining my driver's license was no longer only about me and my freedom. I realized that with this privilege came the potential to impact other people's lives significantly—including negatively.

The drive home was intense. At one point, I misunderstood the lines on the road and had to swerve back in my lane to avoid oncoming traffic. Drivers honking behind me weren't aware that I wasn't legitimately a driver yet and shouldn't be compared to other experienced drivers on the road. I was learning. I did pretty well for a first-time driver, if I do say so myself! It goes to show we never know where anyone is on

> We need to *permit* others, and ourselves, to have plenty of grace.

their journey of life. Perhaps they just got their permit. It reminds me how we need to *permit* others, and ourselves, to have plenty of grace.

Over the next six months of practice, driving school, and acquired experience, my skills improved significantly, and I passed my driver's test. Though I acquired a valid driver's license, it's important to note that the official plastic card didn't automatically improve my driving (and I still don't always measure up in other drivers' eyes). Today, despite having my license, the head knowledge, and thousands of hours of experience—I'm still making mistakes. I've veered off the road. I get honked at sometimes. I've even rear-ended a couple of cars in my past couple of decades of driving (oops!).

When you follow the process and work out your Innovated Identity, you'll still be imperfect, and you won't measure up in everyone's minds. Nor will other people going through their life journey do things right or measure up perfectly to who they're created to be. We all need to give and receive grace. Let's all look past the infractions and mistakes that offend us, so we can see the person behind the wheel.

We can measure up and win, but we have to stop using our world of Comparison as the benchmark to measure up to. When our world expects us to give Comparison the keys while we sit passively in the passenger seat hoping to measure up and win . . . we know now that it won't happen! If you continue to live your life trying to measure up and win the way our culture has taught you, not only will you never win—you'll never really live your life.

When you're too busy trying to fulfill everyone else's expectations for who they think you should be—acting and looking how they want, saying what they think you should say, and acquiring what they think you should have—you're not becoming who you were created to be and will never fully get to do what you were designed to do. Take it from me, a former professional Comparaholic—you'll be the winner of . . . nothing.

Instead, think of obtaining your learner's permit as the groundwork necessary for obtaining your valid driver's license (aka *Innovated Identity*), beginning with going through some of the self-exploration questions.

Others' Exploration.

Studying for your learner's permit will include taking a close look at who and what you've been admiring and attempting to be thus far. This is where the self-exploration merges with others-exploration.

Here are a few questions to get you started learning more about yourself through others':

- Who do I want to be like, or wish I could imitate?
- Who comes to mind when I think of someone that has a so-called perfect life? A celebrity, industry leader, competitor, coworker, family member, a friend, or maybe an enemy?
- Who do I compare myself to most often? What type of person?
- What groups or associations have I wanted to measure up to?
- If I could be mistaken for anyone else, who would I want it to be?

Let's talk about mistaken identities for a moment.

Most of us have had a mistaken identity at some point. Doesn't everyone have a doppelganger? I've had many. Something about my red hair seems to make people think that I look like every other redhead in the world. Growing up, there were only two redheads in my elementary school: a girl named Amber and me. The principal knew us apart, but for some reason, he enjoyed teasing me by calling me Amber. I hated it. It made me feel like I didn't have my own identity—like a mistaken identity. I was so bothered that my parents finally had a talk with the principal asking him to stop.

My principal was being playful, yet I felt hurt and like I didn't matter. People can experience the same feelings when they are truly mistaken for someone else. This typically isn't deliberate or intentionally harmful. It's actually due to the same cognitive phenomenon that causes people of one ethnicity to think that people of a different ethnicity all look alike. It's called the *other-race effect* (ORE), which states it scientifically makes it harder for people of one race to readily recognize or identify individuals of another.[24] It's the reason that non-Asians might think that all Asians look alike. While many people call it racism or bigotry (and the media tends to capitalize on this), it's actually due to an individual's lack of familiarity and exposure paired with the human brain's limitations.

Siblings and twins get their fair share of mistaken identity. Ever met a set of twins and thought, *How in the world do people tell them apart?* As you get to know them individually, you also begin to recognize the physical differentiation—even in identical twins. In order for our brains to overcome the other-race effect, we need to continue to make effort interacting and getting to know people that are not like us.

So, no—I'm not Amber, nor Julianne Moore, Molly Ringwald, Nicole Kidman, nor any of the other redheads for whom I've been mistaken.

All of these mistaken identities and the related comparisons are due to fundamental similarities or differences. I didn't choose my hair color to be different than most, siblings don't intend to look like another sibling, and people of Asian descent don't pick features that look similar to those who share the same geographic region.

While it can annoy us at times or make us feel disrespected—like we don't have our own separate identity—it's important to recognize that these mistaken identities happen naturally without inherently wrong intentions.

On the other hand, mistaken identities *can* cause us harm when we mistake our own identity. This can happen when we want to be like someone else due to thinking so highly of them or wanting what they have. Sometimes it goes further, and we want to *be* them. That is what I want you to focus on right now: the internal mistaken identities.

When I was six years old, Disney's *The Little Mermaid* came out. I watched the movie over and over and was mesmerized by Ariel. She had red hair, like mine, though hers looked better (I wanted to know how she got her perfect '80s rainbow bangs to look like that—the fork thing never worked for me!). Not only was she beautiful, but I loved her voice.

Yes, I realize Ariel was animated and not a real person, but try telling that to a six year-old. She was real to me, and in the 90-minutes of screen-time I got to know her, I really wanted to be her. My friends and I hosted singing contests to see who was more like Ariel (of course, I always won).

Adults do this, too. From afar, we watch movie stars, our favorite singers or influencers—wishing we could *be* them. Obsessing over their perfect life of fame and fortune, we see only a glimpse by following them on the news, social media, or through brief moments we have seen or interacted with them. We don't see the full picture. *New York Times* best-selling author, Steve Furtick, wisely said, "The reason we struggle with insecurity is because we compare our behind-the-scenes with everyone else's highlight reel."

We don't see our idols behind-the-scenes. Their bloopers happen out of our view and we don't know their real-life struggles, short-comings, or what they sacrifice to have the qualities we admire. We don't know their desires—they may long for what you have. We only see their edited highlight reels (and they're often fake). The same goes for everyday people, not just idols.

We all have someone or a group of people that come to mind when we think, "If only I was her or I could be like them". When Sima Vasa, one of the youngest division presidents at a market research company, found herself reading an article about moms who had incredible careers, she wondered what she was doing wrong. She was struggling to be the mom she wanted to be. One day she realized that she wasn't seeing the women behind the article; she had no idea what their relationships were like. "I didn't take myself out of the game. I took control of my life!" Sima said in an interview with Forbes.[25] Instead of continuing to live a life that wasn't suited for her, she resigned from her job and innovated her identity to be who she was created to be.

Who are these people for you? Perhaps it's the PTO president who looks all put together, heads up every fundraiser, and who is well-liked and respected by all. Or maybe it's your superior at the office who has the title, the prestige, the paycheck, and leaves no head unturned with every click of her high heeled shoes.

These people and attributes can be great, but are we seeing the whole picture?

Of course not.

There are no perfect lives. Often, we see people at the peak of their fame committing suicide, suffering from depression, or on the news in the latest scandal. It may appear from the outside that someone has everything we want and has it all, but it's a myth.

Myth or not, I want you to hang out in that space for a bit longer. I want you to think of that person or persons you theoretically believe you'd want to be, and let's take it a step further. What specific attributes about that person draw you to them?

I'll use my silly childhood obsession with Ariel as an example:

Her hair. I already shared with you how much I longed for her perfect hair. It was smooth and flawless (even underwater!). I saw my hair as frizzy, messy, and undesirable. She made red hair look good when my red hair wasn't a positive attribute in grade school. Back in the late '80s and early '90s, perfect bangs were all the rage. We'd comb them over to one side and poof them up. The higher, the better. Ariel always had effortlessly perfect bangs. While I spent hours as a kid in front of a mirror with bottles of Aqua Net® trying to achieve even a portion of that perfection, she ran a fork through her hair. Not to mention, she was pretty and had a perfect smile.

Then there was her voice. Singing and music have been a big part of my life. When asked what I wanted to be when I grew up, a singer was first on my list. While I've always been able to carry a tune and have taken voice lessons, the extent of my singing career was solos in high school and singing with the church praise teams. I don't have an American Idol-worthy voice to make me quit my day job.

Now that I've identified what got Comparison's attention and sparked my envy of Ariel, let's unravel this a bit further: *Why* did I want those attributes?

What would her hair, looks, and voice offer me if I miraculously obtained them?

We know that comparing her hair and beauty caused me to stop at the appearance roadblock, and her fantastic voice would be a skill, or a talent, categorized under the roadblock of achievements.

When I think through the *Deserted Island* test, I can identify that the only real reason for wanting beautiful hair had to do with how others perceived me. I wanted to keep up with the trends, and if no one were around, it wouldn't have mattered if my bangs measured up like Ariel's. I can also conclude that, while having a pleasant voice like hers would be great, even if I was singing alone in the shower, ultimately, when I'm downright honest, I wanted her voice so I could stand out and sound better than others. I wanted to be famous on the radio and TV. I wanted to be known. What little girl doesn't? But let's be real, little girls aren't alone in having these longings.

Real-Life Implementation.

This process can be taken further than childhood dreams and mermaids. It may not be big bangs and a voice for radio; the longings may be more realistic and subtle. Let's look at an example of how this can be practically implemented into our adult lives.

A coaching client of mine named Lonnie was successfully building her own business as a dietician. Her philosophy of helping her clients change their mindset toward food to help them reach their goals was very intriguing. As we talked, she began telling me about a local competitor she followed. This woman's brand awareness was growing rather quickly, and Lonnie saw that she was going to be speaking at a big convention in Chicago.

"It's not fair! I'm working just as hard in my business, and yet she's invited to speak at this big convention. Why wasn't I invited to speak?"

Comparison was currently in control of the situation.

"What do you like about traveling and speaking?" I asked.

She thought for a minute, then said, "Actually, I don't really enjoy traveling—it doesn't fit well into my current lifestyle."

Chatting further, she realized she wasn't even passionate about speaking in front of huge groups of people.

So, I asked her, "What is it that this woman has that you wish you could have?"

Ultimately, it was her following and the recognition. These desires aren't wrong—we are all motivated in different ways.

Because Comparison was in control and manipulating Lonnie's thinking, she incorrectly assessed what to do with the information about her competitor. Lonnie was associating speaking at a conference as a necessary achievement and she felt unnecessarily inadequate.

Lonnie needed to realize that she could measure up and win in her profession and start by weighing the cost that Comparison was having on her life. For every minute Lonnie put into researching, comparing, and being envious of her competitor, she was losing time and energy to focus on her own business and help her clients. Comparison needed to be put in its proper place.

Next, Lonnie needed to innovate her identity. She had already identified who she *wanted* to be and extrapolated the characteristics and meaning behind *why*. Now we could properly utilize Comparison to help us uncover more of who Lonnie was created to be and then help her do what she's designed to do—and do it better.

What do I mean by this?

Lonnie wasn't created to be a duplicate of her competitor or to do exactly what her competition was doing. After all, there's no need for two of the same people on Earth. The world needs to hear Lonnie's experiences and her way of relaying her message—not a copy of someone else. When Lonnie noticed a characteristic that she admired in someone else, instead of thinking, *they have something I don't, and therefore, I don't measure up,* she needed to explore that specific trait and evaluate whether or not it belonged in her Innovated Identity.

It didn't, so Lonnie let go of the lie that she didn't measure up to her competitor. She realized that, in fact, speaking in Chicago would have taken her away from her current goals!

Because the recognition Lonnie craved is a direct result of helping people, we discovered an innovative way she could help more people that better aligned with her true identity: offering an online course. This would provide the opportunity to impact people all over the world, without the expectations and responsibilities that come from speaking and traveling.

Lonnie could better navigate her journey by limiting what she allows to enter into her sphere so she wouldn't get stuck focusing on others.

When we allow Comparison to take the wheel, we become blind to the value we have to offer the world and we lose focus on where we want to go. Being *you* may look different than you think it should, but the world needs the *real you*.

Comparison is in control when we fail to distinguish between liking someone's characteristics and wanting *to be* that someone. After you identify the people you idolize and discover the reasons why you envy, admire, or desire to be that person, you can look deeper into yourself and gain knowledge to step further into the Innovated Identity we were created to have.

So, now that you have some people in mind to which you compare yourself, begin to extrapolate the characteristics that are the underlying factors attracting you to them. Be honest; don't hold back. This exercise will help reveal some directional points for when you innovate your identity in the next chapter.

Perhaps ask yourself questions like:

- What about this person makes me want to be like them? Does it have to do with their assets, appearance, or achievements?
- What would I stand to gain if I were this person, had what they had, or obtained their characteristics? How would my life be improved?
- In what ways am I different than the qualities I admire in them?

You may learn new insight about yourself—some of which may catch you off guard. For instance, perhaps this exercise revealed that you compare yourself to other women because of physical appearance. You may think, "I wish I were a supermodel—how can that be beneficial?"

You're not alone. So many of us women struggle with body image. As we learned in Chapter Three, our world primes us to think this way, and it's likely a lifelong struggle—but one that you can win. You must make up your mind ahead of time and choose the mindset of a winner. Don't give up; answer the same questions. They may reveal something new to you.

Identify the type of women to whom you compare yourself (fitness models? *Playboy* models? Thinner or curvier gals? Darker or lighter-skinned women?)

What specifically in your life would improve if you obtained what you wish you had?

You may think you'd feel sexier or more attractive if you looked a certain way, but I'm asking you to go further: what would feeling sexier do for you? What would it result in? Perhaps you'd attract more men. If so, is that what you want? Are you single and looking for a spouse? Are you craving the attention you think this physical change would bring? If yes, would that attention be for the right reasons? While many women do enjoy being noticed, most women admit to feeling empty and visually taken advantage of when men gaze at them or only appreciate them for their bodies. It's a pervasive tension women face—wanting to feel pretty or attractive, but also wanting to be appreciated for more than our physical appearance.

Do you think you will be more welcomed and accepted into groups of other women? Again, take the thought further: If this is the case, what would this gain you, and are the women who would welcome you because of your appearance the type of women who would add significance to your life? Or would this lead you into the vicious cycle of having to measure up continuously to feel included?

One overweight woman confessed she compares herself to women who are thin because they are confident and powerful. I've heard other women who are overweight say they feel they're not taken seriously and aren't viewed as professional or smart on account of the extra pounds. If this is the case, what is the underlying insecurity?

We want validation. We want acceptance from others. We want to love ourselves.

Dig deep to reveal the underlying reasons you catch yourself comparing yourself to another person. Whether it's the desire for a spouse or friends, social acceptance, power, confidence, or something else, it's time to develop and innovate your identity. Wanting to be seen as attractive, accomplished, or financially successful isn't wrong, but putting too much focus on any of these areas means it's time for an identity tune up.

Your identity reflects your values. What you desire in others often reveals what you value in life. If you are coming to realize that you value sex appeal to a great extent, perhaps this underlying value of acceptance is misaligned and can be altered in your Innovated Identity.

Not only do we compare ourselves to specific people, but also expectations we put on ourselves and those that people and society place on us. Just as we identify who we want to be like, we must recognize the expectations we want to adhere to as well. I agree with the author, speaker, and podcast host, Colin Wright, who said, "It's not your responsibility to want the life that others want for you." Let me follow it up with this: it *is* your responsibility to identify the life you genuinely want and believe is for you.

In my early twenties, I noticed Comparison becoming a significant player in my life. Of course, it was present before then, but it was at this point when I began to believe Comparison's manipulative whispers telling me I didn't measure up to the world's expectations. Striving to live up to unmet expectations is similar to wanting to be another person.

Seeds of cultural expectations are planted in our brains during life experiences. Some of those seeds were planted in my mind when adolescent male abusers tried to force me to do what I wasn't comfortable doing and through a boyfriend's struggle with pornography that led me to feel like even the really good guys only find specific types of women appealing. Even in some of the teachings in my psychology studies in college—if I didn't have *that* look or the *right* irresistible personality, then I don't measure up.

Those seeds were further cultivated in my marriage. While my husband didn't say anything wrong or intend any harm, I internalized statements he made. My thinking shifted inward, I paid more attention to my appearance, and I was dissatisfied. I believed I wasn't good enough for him—that he wished I looked different and was a better wife. A simple comment, like that a woman had gained weight, or a well-meaning comment like, "that dress doesn't look good on you" became distorted in my mind and I thought, *If I ever gain weight then he won't find me attractive or, The model in the catalog looked good in the dress, why can't I measure up?"*

My focus was on myself. My values changed from feeling that appearance wasn't important to it becoming an idol in my life. Until I tuned-up my values, and tuned-in to what was important, I couldn't be in control over Comparison. I needed to change who I wanted to be like and the expectations I was valuing. But how?

That's where the Innovated Identity came in.

Hopefully, you've done some self-exploration and others-exploration and have extrapolated some new knowledge. Gaining this knowledge is like studying for your learner's permit so you can eventually obtain the experience needed to grow into your new, Innovated Identity.

Much of what you've thought you wanted up until now won't serve you in the future the way you once perceived. Perhaps the people you've been comparing yourself to will change as you examine your values. It's ok. Don't judge yourself or your past—give grace for swerving over the lines a little. That's part of the learning process; we all do it as we discover who we were created to be (and even after). Now, let's get down to the creative and intellectual process and start innovating your new identity!

On a scale of 1 to 10, how excited are you to innovate your identity?

(I can't wait!) 1 2 3 4 5 6 7 8 9 10 (I'm dreading it)

CHAPTER EIGHT

This is Me: How can I measure up?

> **Measure up** (v)
> 1. To have necessary or fitting qualifications–often used with to
> 2. To be the equal (as in ability)

On March 13, 1989, Rita and Guadalupe Velásquez welcomed their firstborn into the world in Austin, Texas. Born four weeks early and weighing only 2 pounds 10 oz, they named their baby girl Elizabeth Anne Velásquez or "Lizzie" for short. The doctors told the Velásquezes that Lizzie was born with an extremely rare congenital disease that would prevent her from accumulating body fat or gaining weight. They also warned Lizzie's parents that she probably would never be able to crawl, walk, talk, or do much of anything without assistance.[26]

Imagine receiving that news as a new parent. All of your hopes for that first word, first step, the first day of school—vanished into thin air. I can picture how they felt walking down the maternity hall and seeing other new parents holding their babies; how strong the temptation would be to compare the futures of other newborns with Lizzie's presumed life ahead.

But the Velásquezes did no such thing. Lizzie's parents chose not to look at what the world's standard for measuring up was; instead, they measured up to *win*. They told the doctors they would go home and love their beautiful baby the same way they would have had she been born without the unfavorable prognosis, and they would take care of her to the best of their ability.

And that's exactly what they did.

While little Lizzie was unable to gain weight and had the use of only one eye, the doctors were wrong about her future abilities. Driving forward several years, her parents had the joy of hearing her first words, seeing her first steps, and waving on her first day of school—and Lizzie had no idea she was any different from her peers. When a classmate made some unkind comments, Lizzie asked her parents why that boy was rude to her and why he said those things. She wanted to know what was different about her. They replied, "The only thing that is different about you, Lizzie, is that you are smaller than the other children. But never let that define you."[27]

So, she didn't.

Lizzie continued to be her awesome fun self, and carried on with her life, never allowing her different appearance to change her. However, when Lizzie was in high school, she discovered an eight-second video on YouTube with 4 million views and thousands of comments that altered her life. The video included a picture of Lizzie, labeling her the "Ugliest Woman in the World."[28]

As if that weren't enough to send any 17-year-old girl into a whirlwind of emotions, the comments were so horrible that I can barely even stand to type them here—things like, "Kill it with fire," "Please put a gun to your head and kill yourself," and "Why did your parents keep you?"

I've known about Lizzie's story for over a year now, but my eyes still tear up as I write this. I cannot imagine the excruciating pain Lizzie experienced as she read those hateful comments. How can human beings be so incredibly mean to one another? Many people would give up and hand their keys to Comparison—sometimes for it to drive them to deep depression or even suicide. Lizzie was tempted to retaliate as she felt what was happening inside of her but chose to take control over comparison and *win* instead. She walked away from the video and used the defining moment to her advantage by asking herself some important questions.

By this point she was well aware of her different appearance, but did anything about her appearance ever truly define her? No.

What was true in this situation? The truth was that she was grateful! She might not be able to see out of one of her eyes, but she can see out of the other!

She thought about what her focus was going to be—should she focus on her health being not so great, or should she focus on having great hair?

She could not—and would not—allow the people who called her a monster to define her. So, what would she measure up to? It wasn't going to be what the world said her identity should be—she innovated her identity.

"This is me!"

Lizzie's defining moment arose out of evil intent and sparked a future she would never have imagine existed. She is now a motivational speaker, a published author of three books, and an anti-bullying activist hosting a YouTube channel with nearly a million subscribers. Her

TEDTalk® entitled "How do You Define Yourself?" has had nearly 10 million views.[29] Lizzie's choice to claim control over Comparison in her life has given her a life of joy, purpose, and impact. She helps other girls innovate their identity in her own way.

Of course, life isn't perfect for Lizzie, and she is very authentic with her audience. Measuring up to win requires authenticity, not perfection. Her health waivers, she will never gain weight, and it's not always easy for Lizzie knowing that she looks different. She's often asked how she can stay so positive. Her response? "I allow myself sad days to be alone and close the blinds and listen to sad music like Adele and cry, eat junk food, and have a pity party. I let it out of my system for one day, but the sun comes out the next day. I have the power to go on."[30]

Most likely, you've never had your appearance publicly ridiculed via video for the world to see. You may or may not have ever dealt with the comparison issues that accompany being a parent. However, I know you can relate with this story on some level because we all have our Comparison demons—and I know you want to measure up and *win*.

Lizzie and her parents each weighed their cost to giving Comparison control. Rita and Guadalupe knew they were not in for an easy road in this World of Comparison as parents of a differently-abled child. Being a differently-appearing girl growing up in this world also came with its challenges for Lizzie. Nonetheless, they looked at their options and saw that allowing Comparison to be the driver would result in costs that weren't worth it to them—they made their decision.

Then, whether they realized it or not, they innovated their identities. I doubt Rita and Guadalupe talked about what their identity would look like in the future or had a chat prior to conceiving their child saying, "Part of my Innovated Identity is unconditional love," but regardless, it was already a part of their identity, and they made the choice to put it to work.

The same was true for Lizzie. When feeling Comparison tugging at her life, she went searching for the truth about who she was created to be. Lizzie found gratitude, purpose, and beauty beyond physical appearance to measure up to as her identity.

Our Innovated Identity.

We need to have a clear and stable source against which to measure ourselves. If we try to measure up to people, to our own conceptualized standards and expectations or to those that others want for us, we will never win. Instead, we'll be exhausted and unfulfilled. In order to win in this world of Comparison, we must continue to innovate our own identity so we can benchmark against it instead of comparing ourselves to other people (or even to our past or current selves).

We'll continue to unwrap this concept of innovating our identity further, but as a quick review: our Innovated Identity is developed when we assess the valuable attributes of our present identity, refine them, and add in the traits that align with who we were created to be. The outcome of our Innovated Identity is a positive benchmark that we can measure ourselves against and measure up to instead of attempting to measure up to the world's ever-changing and superficial standards. While you shouldn't expect to measure up to your Innovated Identity 100% of the time, it represents an overall picture of what you've come to know about whom you were created to be—a conglomeration of all your real and desired attributes rolled up into one.

Knowing who you are and liking that person will help get you on the road to measuring up and winning.

Whose Voice Matters?

When innovating your identity, you need to be mindful of what voices you are listening to and decide which matter. Even our internal voices can deceive us. Note: our Innovated Identity is always positive. God didn't make junk. Yes, we all have weaknesses that we can improve on, but we started out from a place of worth and value. Don't allow anything less to be projected onto you.

The next time you notice you are comparing yourself to someone or something (which by now, I hope you are recognizing this far more often), isolate the thought and attempt to find the root cause behind the comparison that was made. For example, when a friend stops by unannounced and sees my house in complete disarray, my mind could think, *How embarrassing; my house is a wreck! Loads of laundry all over the couch, dirty dishes in the sink—she's going to think I'm a slob. Maybe she's right, am I a slob? My home should look better—her house always looks in perfect order. She has it all together and then there's me, the slob.*

My internal dialogue somehow made being a slob a part of my identity, and I didn't measure up to my orderly friend. Is this an accurate statement? And even more importantly, does it even matter? We make quick assumptions about situations and think, *I don't measure up to them (or they probably think I don't measure up to them). She's a better mom/wife/whatever.*

Meanwhile, we don't stop to think about whether we should even care about what *they* think of us. Should I worry about that person's opinion of me and whether or not I measure up to them? What significance does their opinion play in our lives? If, for some reason, my friend actually thinks I'm a slob (which I highly doubt), does that change who I am—my identity?

Nope.

My messy house is between my family and me, and if she imparts judgment on me, then I need to consider who I'm allowing to speak into my life.

Back to the point—she never said I was a slob—*I did.*

I made the entire rant up in my head and went on a mental tirade, worrying about what she might think. The root of that comparison was my critical internal voice that also shouldn't have mattered because it wasn't using Comparison in a valuable way; instead, it allowed Comparison to control me in the opposite direction of my Innovated Identity.

On the other hand, if neat and orderly should be a part of my Innovated Identity because it's important to *me*, that's something I can work at and improve upon.

So many times, measuring up to other people isn't even in the equation. Yet, I sit pouting in the passenger seat while Comparison drives me the wrong way down a one-way street.

Removing what doesn't belong.

Why do we do this? Why do we let Comparison take control? It's often due to our people-pleasing, perfectionist (sometimes selfish) human tendencies. Or maybe we can go as far as to call it what it is: pride.

Does your current identity have any of that? Mine did. My prideful tendencies became more evident through the self-exploration and innovation process. I soon came to realize that I wasn't created to be a people pleaser—self-seeking pride doesn't fit well in *anyone's* Innovated Identity. We should discard anything in our current identity that doesn't belong. When I removed *pride* and *people-pleasing*, it didn't immediately take away the tendency; however, it gives me permission to reconfigure my thoughts and actions to line up with my Innovated Identity.

Last year, a gentleman saw a video of me on social media. He invited me into his invitation-only online group geared toward professionals reciprocating online support for their work and content. After joining, I realized that I was a small fish in a big pond, and this invitation was an honor. The group consisted of approximately fifty professionals from around the world that I had never met and about whom I knew little. Initially, Comparison played the appropriate role in helping me learn how to acclimate and become involved in the group. Since no documented rules and procedures existed, I watched what other experienced members were creating, and how often they posted. Then I compared what I was doing already and learned what I could do differently.

All went well until I started giving Comparison a bit too much control. Many of these professionals had talent, skill, and experience in an arena to which I was somewhat new. They invested time and energy. Some had livelihoods riding on how well their content was received, whereas I was not dependent on the same metric. Now I see how I was like a frog in a cold pot: as Comparison started taking control over my mind, slowly turning up the heat, it prompted me to create as often as other members did, gain as much engagement as they had, and impress them with my quick growth. The people pleaser in me emerged as I gave Comparison more control. I wanted to be accepted so I gave more of my time and mental capacity to the group, which in turn caused other areas in my life to suffer. I was crashing into the Achievements roadblock and needed to evaluate who or what I was trying to measure up to, and why.

Thankfully, I had already innovated my identity and had a clear, stable measuring stick by which to evaluate this situation so I could adequately measure up, instead of trying to measure up to other people. It didn't take long to realize my motives were pride based, conflicting with my Innovated Identity. Gaining the approval of and impressing a bunch of strangers by exceeding group requirements wasn't worth what it cost me in time, energy, anxiety and neglect of my personal life. Once I realigned my perspective with my Innovated Identity and gave up trying to be the best group member, I was back to winning.

Should I Compare Myself to Me?

When people learn that I speak on the topic of Comparison, a common retort I've heard is, "You need to compete with yourself instead of other people."

I'm usually able to repress my gut response to grin and reply with, "And how is that working for you?"

While I understand the sentiment behind the thought of comparing against the self, I disagree with the outcome. You see, we still tend to give Comparison control when competing against ourselves and our personal expectations. Because Comparison is natural to our being—knitted into our DNA and here to stay—we do, in fact, need a helpful benchmark to which we can compare ourselves. However, simply looking at ourselves will not prove a useful measurement. In fact, it can be highly detrimental and produce a negative impact when we rely on competing against our present or past selves. It may seem like a positive solution because when you compete with yourself, then you're not thinking poorly of anyone else. *I'm trying to improve.* But there are drawbacks.

We are already so hard on ourselves. Women using themselves as a measuring stick often become their own worst enemies. In some ways, they may never be able to measure up to what they remember as their past selves, which can lead to resentment of their present selves. Here are a few simple illustrations: As for appearance, when I was 25 years old, I had no problem losing love handles when they happened to sneak a ride on my sides. A decade later, there's no way that I can measure up to the same me with my former metabolism that made rebounding back to skinny life so fast and easy. According to peers a decade or two ahead of me who've undergone that wonderful experience called menopause, it's possible I may never fit into that same pair of jeans.

Regarding my abilities and achievements—who knows? Achieving or surpassing the same athletic performance or academic accomplishments may look altogether different. My current and past assets may change, as well. No matter how much I really love that adorable pair of sparkly 6-inch stilettos, there may come a time where owning (or at least utilizing) them may not be in my future asset mix, and that sporty two-door coupe may no longer be practical. As technology changes and becomes outdated, the amazing skills you had in the past may no longer be necessary, which may lead to job loss. Change is inevitable—and not always in the direction that the world of Comparison thinks is beneficial for measuring up to its standards.

The future is unknown and partially out of our control, so if we compete and compare ourselves against ourselves in expectation of what we think should happen, it may result in undervaluing and limiting ourselves— or the complete opposite. We may overestimate our capacity and put unwarranted pressure on ourselves to achieve the unattainable. Either way, there's a better way than to use ourselves as the benchmark to measure up.

We already know our identity is not something determined by our Appearances, Assets, or Achievements. While they do play a part in shaping who we are, we are continually growing, maturing, and becoming who we were created and put on this Earth to be; so shouldn't the measuring stick we use to compare ourselves to also reflect that evolution?

This is where our Innovated Identity comes in to play. The best alternative to comparing ourselves to other people or expectations is not to compare ourselves to our present or past selves, but to innovate our current self and create our Innovated Identity to measure up to.

Characteristics of Others.

We covered the first step in innovating your identity by identifying the attributes in other people you admire. In the last chapter, you recognized some of the individuals and ideas you've placed on a pedestal—maybe even someone that you have idolized to the point of wishing you could be them. Hopefully, you identified *why* you think highly of them. Coming back to the reality that they—in and of themselves—are not perfect, nor would being them lead you to a life of perfection or satisfaction.

Now, let's take the characteristics you admire about each of those people and factor them into our equation one by one, asking ourselves the question: *Would this attribute make sense in my life, and should it be included in my identity?*

Though I've gone through this innovation process, I'm regularly re-evaluating and innovating my identity as I grow and learn more about myself.

One of the people I've looked up to and admired is a woman named Melissa Spoelstra. Melissa has been a mentor and a valued friend to me for many years. Her life experience precedes mine by about a decade. She's a respected leader who serves her local community and is also a highly esteemed published author and international speaker. If I didn't have the privilege of knowing her so well, from the outside looking in, I'd probably think she was perfect. While I've never given Comparison control to the point that I wished to be her, there are many of her attributes that I respect and can extrapolate as I innovate my own identity.

Here are a few of her attributes I admire:

- She's a giver who sacrifices her time, energy, and money to help others
- She steps out in faith and is obedient to her higher calling
- She's eager to learn and embraces humility
- She sees the good in people yet is also wise and discerning
- She is gifted at writing and speaking and utilizes these talents to impact others
- She's bold and confident and speaks the truth in love
- She's genuine and authentic and doesn't hide behind masks

Each of these characteristics lines up with who I was created to be. Though I haven't completely grown into it yet, I've added them into my Innovated Identity. Some of these attributes are universal for everyone to implement, like humility and discernment.

By comparing aspects of my current identity to the qualities I admire in my friend, I'm doing what is called *benchmarking*—one of the ways Comparison is helpful while innovating my identity. As beneficial as benchmarking can be, it can also be a slippery slope. I need to be ultra-careful to keep hold of my wheel, so Comparison doesn't take over and drive away with my thoughts. I don't want to measure myself against and compare myself to Melissa.

The goal with this process is to take a glance out the window of your life and open up your eyes to what you should include in your Innovated Identity. Still, the focus cannot stay out the window—take a glance and a mental note, glean what you can, then focus through the windshield of your own life toward your destination.

There were other attributes I admire about Melissa that I didn't add, because they don't fit with who I am created to be. For instance, she's a brilliant teacher, gifted at explaining complex ideas in an easy to understand manner. This isn't one of my natural gifts. She's an intellectual that loves to delve into the deepest parts of a topic, down to the original language and context. She loves studying books that I find boring. As much as I love to read, research, and learn, her intellectual characteristics don't belong in my Innovated Identity. I wasn't created to teach the same way Melissa is—and that's ok! My goal is not to become her or measure up to her, but to measure up to my own Innovated Identity. When there's an attribute that we wish we could have but never will, instead of comparing ourselves, we should celebrate how others are created and how their attributes help them excel in doing what they're designed to do!

While Melissa is a friend and mentor who I highly respect, like any other human being, she's not perfect. No one is perfect—a major reason why we should never use another human being (including ourselves) as a final benchmark or measuring stick for who we want to be.

Another reason to avoid measuring up to others is that each individual has so much to bring to the world. If I put my focus and energy into trying to be a replica of Melissa, I would rob the world of what I was created to bring. My unique flair and way of contributing would be lost if I focused on trying to imitate her. The differences that make me who I am will resonate with people who may have never taken a second glance at Melissa, and vice versa. As much as our world strives to make everyone the same, deep down, we crave innovation and enjoy seeing full potential released. There's a reason we love to watch shows like *American Idol* and *The Biggest Loser.* We love observing the contestant's journey through personal growth, development, and differentiating themselves as they blossom into their unique selves. Hugh Jackman said it well as P.T. Barnum in the film *The Greatest Showman:* "No one ever made a difference by being like everyone else."

Allow yourself to have the same license for creativity, innovation, and expression that you extend to everyone else.

Purpose, Passion, and Talents.

In addition to working through the characteristics of others we admire, innovating your identity requires identifying your talents and passions. They need not be what are currently being expressed or ones we've fully cultivated (though include those as well). They can be little sparks that you feel deep down. Start by making a list of what intrigues you. If you get stuck, reach out to people who love you and know you well as they may enlighten you to aspects about yourself that you have never realized. This exercise may reveal your purpose, or a calling may emerge. Identity discovery often precedes uncovering life purpose, so if your passions fail to come easy, don't fret. My theory for why this is true is that our purpose is typically the way we execute our Innovated Identity. Once we know who we were created to be, we can then do what we are designed to do. Our Innovated Identity gives us the proper benchmark, so we are no longer sidetracked, distracted, or confused by the world around us—we can move forward in response. We may already have glimpses of our *why* well before we innovate our identity. Many of us are already aware of overarching purposes that are part of who we are. Keep those in mind and include them on your list.

Your faith and value system is worth exploring while contemplating your purpose. As for me, I don't care for the term 'religious' and I use the label 'Christian' hesitantly because of the negative connotations it can carry—my faith is comprised of my personal relationship with Jesus, my Savior. This relationship drives my passion and purpose since one of the overarching purposes in my life is to become more like Him. I've discovered more about my purpose by studying Him.

I feel compelled to love people as He did—showing others they are loved and valued by God is part of my purpose for being on Earth. Jesus is my primary benchmark for discovering my Innovated Identity, along with my innate qualities and those I've identified from others. The more I study His life, the more I realize that He embodies many of the attributes on my growing index of innovations. I couldn't innovate my identity without my faith.

My natural personality and talents play a huge part in my transformation while innovating my identity. Some undeniable threads have run through my life for as long as I can remember. For example, I am an extrovert, and I thoroughly enjoy interacting with people and helping them. Though I still enjoy my alone time, I go crazy when I'm not around people for extended periods. I even enjoy people watching (which may explain why I knew I would study psychology in college). I've always had a deep desire to connect people, and I excel at it. I'm known for being a connector—another attribute in my Innovated Identity.

As you continue this process of cautiously benchmarking against people you admire—compiling values, passions, and purposes that are important to you, and evaluating the natural talents that bring you joy, you'll begin to see a picture of your Innovated Identity. Most likely you'll find that it looks much like who are you already are! It should also excite you to see room for growth, expansion, and development into being what you were created to be—a more innovated version of your current self. It will resonate with you, even if it feels like you're being stretched. No one ever reaches perfection on Earth, and you'll never measure up perfectly to your Innovated Identity—and that's ok! It's built with lots of spandex and stretch for those rough days—a one-size-fits-all for you alone, with lots of grace and coverage. No shame exists when using it as your measuring stick. When we embrace our Innovated Identity and measure up to it instead of the fake ID's the world tells us to measure up to, we'll be less likely to give Comparison control. By learning who we were created to be and what that person looks like, we can measure up properly and win in this world of Comparison!

Though not an exhaustive list, below are some of the pieces that make up my Innovated Identity:

- Bold and confident
- A Truth-teller
- Desire for humility and ongoing growth

- Unfailing love and acceptance—flaws and all
- Faithful and loyal
- Serve others
- Social and outgoing
- Respectful
- Guide others who want to be guided, but not forceful or demanding
- A Connector of people and ideas
- An Advocate for others
- An Encourager
- Light in a dark world
- Successful at what I set my mind on
- A Listener
- Generous
- A Freedom advocate
- Have a heart for children and the next generation
- Supporter of individual rights/human rights
- Healthy and balanced
- Approachable
- A Realistic optimist
- Genuine, Authentic, no masks
- Stand up for what I believe, no matter what anyone thinks

The list continues on as I continue to learn who I am created to be throughout my lifetime. Don't be afraid to write down what comes to mind, even if it seems unusual, elementary, or grammatically incorrect. When it comes to Innovating your Identity, don't be bound by social or grammatical confines. Be you.

As I continue to discover and innovate my identity, I work at growing into that person. I still trip over roadblocks and get detoured from time to time with outside distractions tempting me to hand Comparison the keys. To be brutally honest, some days I don't want to drive the path I know to be best, so I hand the wheel over and let Comparison drive me down the dead-end road that leads to self-pity, discouragement, and despair. However, those rough patches are fewer and farther between, and those days when I feel like giving up are rare (but hey, we're all human).

With our Innovated Identity as our measuring stick, we can better utilize Comparison the way it was intended to be used in our lives instead of the detrimental way that society has trained us to allow it to abuse us.

If you keep working out your Innovated Identity, you will hold in your hand that valid ID. It may not be today, perhaps not even next week, but eventually, you'll be like that proud teenager smiling for the camera after passing their driving test. Instead of holding up a laminated card, you'll be holding your head high—proud to live out the real you. Discovering and innovating your identity helps you become confident, secure, and less worried about what others think. You'll be able to say, "This is me!"

If you're interested in some extra help and resources on discovering your Innovated Identity, check out ComparisonBook.com/resources for additional support. On a scale of 1 to 10, how close do you currently measure up to your Innovated Identity?

(Spitting image) 1 2 3 4 5 6 7 8 9 10 (Long way to go)

PART 3
NAVIGATE YOUR JOURNEY

CHAPTER NINE

Navigating Your Journey: What does it look like to Win?

> **Win** (v)
> Be successful or victorious in (a contest or conflict).
> Synonyms: take, be the victor in, come first in,
> take first prize in, triumph in

If you were to ask a random person what it looks like to measure up and win in life, they might say something like obtain a doctorate degree, reach the top rung of the corporate ladder, marry a *Bachelor* star, or have 2.5 kids, a dog, and the biggest house on the block with a luxury SUV in the garage.

Our Comparison-driven world wants to confine us within specific metrics. However, measuring up and winning has nothing to do with any of the above, nor does it correlate with living in a particular zip code, wearing a single digit pant size, or writing a *New York Times* best-seller.

You'll realize you're measuring up when you've discovered your Innovated Identity. You'll look in the mirror and see an amazing person staring back at you whose innate worth is bursting at the seams with infinite value and potential. Measuring up is when you live out who you're created to be.

Winning is when we choose to unearth and express that potential within. As a wonderful byproduct of being who we are created to be, we get to do what we are designed to do. That always positively impacts our world. Winning equates to doing what we were designed to do.

When I uncovered the truth about Comparison—the good, the bad, and the ugly—I realized I was the one to blame for its power. Comparison is only as powerful as I allow it to be (and I had been giving it way too much power!). When I decreased the control that I gave it over my life, my confidence began to increase. By comparing less, I wasn't losing all the time. I had the power to win all along; I just needed to choose to use it.

It's liberating to discover that winning is a choice you get to make, instead of something that only happens for a lucky few.

Hopefully, you've already completed the first two steps of the roadmap to win.

The *W* and the *I* are essential, but you also can't win without the *N*. The last step to tackle to *win* in this world of Comparison is to *Navigate your Journey*.

While you're changing for the better with the help of your Innovated Identity, the world around you remains the same. You still live in a world ruled by

Comparison—so how can you best navigate the journey with fewer head-on collisions with Comparison?

To navigate means "to plan and direct the route or course of a ship, aircraft, or other form of transportation, especially by using instruments or maps."[31] As we drive down the highway of life, Comparison offers many mirages for us to veer toward; however, if we are aware and have a plan, we can navigate away from and avoid many of the distractions that cause us to lose focus on our destination.

In the same way that sitting behind the wheel of a car doesn't automatically get you to your destination, winning doesn't just happen. Crucial action steps must take place to get you where you're going. Close your eyes for a minute and picture any successful person that comes to mind. Whether it's an Olympic athlete, award-winning entertainer, prosperous Fortune 500 CEO, or a friend that you look up to—what do all successful people have in common?

They weren't born successful.

They didn't wake up and win without doing anything. First, they had to envision their destination, structure, plans, and goals helping them to move toward that vision, and then intentionally act by navigating their life toward success.

The same is true with winning in this world of Comparison—you need to see the vision, devise a plan, and create pathways that navigate you toward your destination. In this chapter, you'll learn practical ways to help you navigate your journey so that you can *win*. Do the work upfront right now—it's so worth it in the end!

GPS.

When leaving for a road trip, before pulling out of the driveway, I enter my destination into the navigation system. I'm so thankful for the invention of GPS! If you're old enough to remember the pre-GPS era without internet access on our phones, you get what I'm talking about. Gone are the days of printing off directions in advance and crossing our fingers for no road construction or other detours, causing us to stray off our printed course. The GPS on my phone intuitively knows information regarding where I'm headed, and it provides me with the best step-by-step direction list. It updates when my route needs to change, and even verbally guides me where to go.

Wouldn't it be nice if we had a GPS for our lives, too?

Imagine how it would list out the facts and guide us step by step so we could make the best decisions to help us reach our destination. In reality, we are often faced with making those decisions with our feelings to guide us instead of facts. Feelings and emotions make it tricky to keep control over Comparison. They're usually subjective, and we often mistake them for facts that confuse us in the moment and trigger a conflict with Comparison.

Your weak spots are magnets for Comparison. If your father said you'd never measure up to anything, whenever you see a woman who exemplifies what your dad considers successful, you'll be vulnerable to Comparison-controlled thinking.

The feeling: You are jealous of a woman and what she portrays.

The fact: The woman has nothing to do with you. The possible negative results:

- You avoid her to avoid dealing with the feelings that surface.
- You mentally revisit past pain and self-sabotage with thoughts of not being enough.
- You project the bitterness you feel onto this innocent woman and miss out on seeing her as another valuable person.
- You disregard your identity and attempt to become her.

If only there was a GPS to guide us down the road of facts versus feelings—a device that could tell us the logical route to keep heading toward our destination instead of taking an emotional detour and a power struggle with Comparison—life would be so much easier! Until it's invented, we can use a little reminder tool to help detect feelings so you can navigate away from roadblocks and toward your Innovated Identity.

Put your situation through this GPS filter: If it makes you feel *Guilty* (I'm not a good enough person/mom/wife/employee, etc.), if you feel like you have to *Pretend* (pretend to be something you're not or act differently to fit in), or if it adds *Stress* to your life (you have feelings of anxiety, wonder if you can measure up, etc.), then Comparison is probably preying on your emotions and you need to work to uncover the facts before making your decision. Discover what is causing the feelings of **G**uilt, **P**retending, or **S**tress. Until you learn why this is happening, you may need to refrain from certain people, alter some activities, or avoid specific situations on your journey. For now, use the GPS tool to identify and navigate around future potential roadblocks that could arise on your path. Bypass or work out those emotional triggers that could take you off course.

If your road trips are anything like mine, outside forces like road construction or an accident ahead can force you to reroute. These times keep me from utilizing auto-pilot mode and listening for my GPS to tell me where to go; instead, I have to think and act quickly. It's important to pay close attention to temporary signs, rough roads, or confusing lanes that are often unmarked. The goal is to get back on track toward my desired destination, but it may take a longer route of side streets with speed bumps or pothole-filled alleys. Eventually, my GPS picks back up and directs me to smooth traveling again.

Comparison threatens to take over like that crater-sized pothole in the middle of an alley that swallows and nearly deflates your tire. It acts like the blinking construction barrels that block your path and sends you on a time-wasting detour. There will be times our GPS fails to connect with the satellites, so we will choose our feelings over the facts and let Comparison drive us where we don't want to go. However, the more experience you gain navigating around potholes and avoiding those barriers, the easier and quicker it gets to resume the path toward your destination by taking control over Comparison.

My major roadblocks were revealed to me a long time ago, and I've been innovating my identity for several years now. While I still run out of gas and stall out occasionally, I run into my roadblocks less and succeed more often than not. I'll never be immune to being hijacked by Comparison, but as long as I follow the WIN Method, I'll keep improving upon my ability to retain control. Recognizing and celebrating each time we succeed is an integral part of navigating our journey. I'm excited to share one of my recent wins with you:

Jenny, a new LinkedIn connection, reached out, and we scheduled a phone call to get better acquainted. She's a bubbly, passionate gal, and I enjoyed learning about her dreams and how I might be of support.

At one point in our conversation, a viral post I had published a few months prior was referenced. This post resonated with many women and was the catalyst for many of my female connections. Intrigued, Jenny asked me to share a link to that post with her. Soon after I shared it, she tagged me in a post that she had allegedly written—it was nearly an exact copy of my popular post. Initially, I was taken aback at the blatant plagiarism and disregard for my intellectual property; I felt violated and used. I concluded that she was looking for a quick way to increase her following by stealing my content that had produced the results she wanted. The more I thought about it, the more my annoyance morphed into a power struggle with Comparison as it begged for control over my mind. *Will her copy of my post get as many views as mine? What if it gets MORE than mine?*

Ugh. I felt that awful feeling. You know that one I'm talking about—the one that's hard to define in words but that no woman can deny as it overtakes you with what feels like a gut-punch. Often prompted by other women, you feel intimidated or threatened in some way—like you won't measure up.

The AAA Method.

When that strange feeling begins to creep in, there's another practical tool you can pull out of your emergency kit to help you navigate back on track. I call it the

AAA Method. Most of us are familiar with the company AAA, a membership service that comes to the rescue for drivers when they get into a tough situation on the road, such as a breakdown or a flat tire.

This AAA method is similar—you have it on hand to use when you notice that deflated or threatened feeling that you can't quite identify or brush off. Here's how you use it:

1. *Ask*

Ask yourself the fundamental questions. What is causing this feeling? Do I feel threatened or intimidated? Am I comparing in any way and how might I be giving Comparison control in this situation?

2. *Acknowledge*

Acknowledge the truth of the situation. If Comparison is driving your thoughts, acknowledge the detrimental impact that may take place with Comparison having control both now and in the future.

3. *Apply*

Apply what you know. Use the practical steps you've learned to regain control over Comparison and apply the truth to the situation. Measure it against your Innovated Identity to help you know if it lines up with who you are, or if Comparison is tempting you to go against your Innovated Identity which may take you off course. Then, *Navigate your Journey* to get back on track.

When I read Jenny's plagiarized post, it left me with that unsettled feeling. Yes, it was wrong of her to steal my content, and it would be reasonable to feel worried or angry, but those weren't the real feelings bothering me; I knew I needed to pull out my *AAA Method*, and fast.

First, I *asked* myself a few questions to uncover what was going on in my mind.

Why am I experiencing this feeling, and what is it?

After thinking deeply and being honest with myself, I realized I felt threatened. I also felt violated that Jenny had claimed my content as if she wrote it. But honestly, if I knew her post would never be seen, I wouldn't be bothered by this situation at all. That information told me that it wasn't the principle of the situation that was bothering me; it was my fear of being compared to Jenny and her receiving more success than I. I felt threatened. I mean, what if she ended up getting more viewers, comments, and engagement on her post than I did on my post?

Next, I *acknowledged* the truth of this feeling— Comparison was trying to take control, and I had a choice to make. Was I going to choose to hand power over to Comparison?

While I felt threatened, I had to apply what I knew to this situation. Though it was wrong of her (whether or not she was aware of what she was doing), I was not going to be harmed by her actions, and there was no logical reason for me to feel threatened. Under most circumstances, intellectual property theft does inflict harm to the victim in some way, but not in this particular case. It wouldn't affect me at all. Sure, Jenny would most likely benefit from something that wasn't hers, but my feeling threatened was unwarranted and was solely a symptom of Comparison driving me crazy. I applied what I knew about the cost; if I continued to give Comparison control, I'd be bitter and awkward toward someone which wouldn't be healthy or result in anything positive. In fact, it would suck my emotional energy and time.

What were my options? I could call her out so that she would be defamed instead of getting fame from stealing my post, but that wouldn't help. I could go into competition mode and strive to beat her at the popularity game, but what trophy would I earn?

When I *applied* what I knew, I realized that her potential success from stealing my work didn't affect me at all. This realization helped me regain control over Comparison instead of letting it control and consume me. I Navigated my Journey and fought the temptation to look at the outcome of her post—my identity isn't dependent on the number of likes or comments I have compared to somebody else. In fact, those numbers have nothing to do with my identity at all! I saved time, stress, and mental effort by choosing to be in charge instead of Comparison.

By using this AAA method and keeping control over comparison, not only did I *win*, but others did as well. I retained my respect and honored my Innovated Identity instead of putting my reputation at risk by getting catty. As time went on, I better got to know Jenny, so I salvaged a friendship. By resolving the matter behind the scenes instead of publicly acting out, I stayed in alignment with that post I wrote for ladies—I acted dignified and with love instead of creating more barriers between women.

I'd be lying if I said it never came to mind again. At first, when Jenny showed up in my newsfeed, my curiosity wanted to know the stats of that silly post—but I'm grateful that I never looked. I navigated my journey to avoid Comparison's traps. I prefer to measure up to my Innovated Identity and win instead of being consumed by the world of Comparison.

Avoiding Comparison Traps.

Let's explore this point further. You've already identified your main Comparison roadblock, now what can we do to decrease the head-on collisions? It doesn't matter if your main Comparison roadblock is Assets, Appearances, or Achievements; you'll never evade Comparison completely. A practical way to decrease the number of times you run into these roadblocks is to avoid the problems that are within your power to sidestep. Structure your life in such a way that you stay away from the obvious traps that can easily entangle you. List the predictable pitfalls that cause Comparison to appear each time you encounter them. You'll continue to improve, and even the less obvious traps will stand out to you as you become more in tune with your Innovated Identity.

We will begin by adjusting and removing some of the stimuli you allow into your sphere. The details will look different for each person, but we can run through some similarities for a jump start. Have your *GPS* (what makes you feel Guilty, want to Pretend, or Stress Out) ready, and use your Innovative Identity as a filter for each of the ideas mentioned below. Don't waste time judging, comparing, or debating with yourself whether you'll miss the items you're about to eliminate from your path. Maybe you'll bring them back in your life someday; perhaps you won't. For now, identify and delete, remove, unfollow, or unsubscribe. The saying "Give me six hours to chop down a tree, and I will spend the first four sharpening the ax"[32] makes perfect sense. Do yourself a favor and spend the time now preparing a clearer path toward your destination.

Think About the *Who* in Your Life.

Pay close attention to the people you focus on and with whom you spend time—friends, neighbors, coworkers, family, a spouse. I'm not suggesting that you start removing people from your life because they chronically tempt you to compare—especially family members or a spouse—but you can control who you spend time with and set boundaries around how you spend time and conversations. Who are the people in your life that spark those Comparison feelings—wishing you had a nicer house or better stuff (Assets), or that you looked prettier, sexier, thinner, or younger (Appearance), or that you had a few marathons under your belt, a more prominent job, or were a better friend or mother (Achievements)? If you're a single person who always hangs with married people, does that act as a potential trap for you to compare relationships? If your fitness instructor pokes fun at how you're still unable to get into that yoga pose or a neighboring male co-worker who is continually pointing out all of the gorgeous women walking by, it's time to get a new instructor or find a way to move desks at your job.

There are people in my life from whom I've had to step back. They weren't bad people, but I didn't like who I became or my mindset when I spent time with them because it wasn't in alignment with my Innovated Identity. Stop hanging out with the proverbial Joneses in your life!

On the opposite end of the spectrum, I've also added some people into my sphere—friends who encourage me and share my values. Some are role models, mentors, and coaches who

> Stop hanging out with the proverbial Joneses in your life!

are in alignment with what my Innovated Identity says will help me measure up, and these friends inspire me to do so. You can identify those people too, and seek out ways to fit them into your life. Motivational speaker Jim Rohn was known for saying, "You are the average of the five people you spend the most time with." When you surround yourself with people who are positive, who value others, who help you avoid roadblocks in your life, and who want the best for you, your journey will be much smoother, and you'll be more likely to reach your destination.

Think About the *What* in Your Life.

Do magazine subscriptions, newsletters, or catalogs arrive in the mail displaying the latest and greatest products, fashion trends, technology, home decor, the vehicle you wish you could own, or detailing the beauty and accomplishments of celebrities who makes you feel like you don't measure up? When I recognized my struggle with Comparison in regard to appearances, I called Victoria's Secret and told them to stop sending me their catalog. Leafing through that thing made me feel so . . . ugly. What comes into your mailbox, email inbox, shopping cart, or pops up as an ad on your laptop may be feeding your mind and giving Comparison control that it shouldn't have.

Social media and online content are areas where we need to get real and raw with ourselves, so we can weed out the traps that are intentionally (and unintentionally) laid before us daily. It's easy to accept Snapchat, Instagram, and Tik Tok as Comparison's playground and follow along because it's normalized in our world. Then there's also the opposite approach—to give up on it, delete your accounts, and shun everything. I'm not here to make you get rid of your beloved social media. In fact, for some of us it's essential for our work or business and we can't delete it. You don't have to give in or give up—but you should do something. Use what you've learned and claim control over Comparison in this massive area of our culture.

Are there podcasts, blogs, or YouTube channels from thought leaders or celebrities that you're subscribed to that cause your mind to wrestle with comparing your accomplishments when you read, hear, or watch the endless success stories? Do the fitness gurus that you follow on Instagram leave you scrutinizing every inch of your body, thinking it's not good enough? When scrolling Facebook, do pictures of your friend's new patio paradise, your girlfriend's vacation pics, and Pottery Barn's promotional ads make you want to call your travel agent or run to a store for retail therapy? Does your latest Netflix binge put your thoughts in the *I wish my life were better* state of mind? When the costs outweigh the benefits, they're a liability in your life.

Unsubscribe. You can always subscribe again later.

Unfollow. You can get your information from another source, and you don't have to unfriend your Facebook connections—unfollow so their posts aren't in your newsfeed. Or, go ahead and unfriend if you need to!

Cancel. Go through your credit card bill looking for unknown Comparison traps that you hadn't realized before. Perhaps cancel dating sites, Netflix, or other memberships for a while, and see what difference this makes in your life.

I give you permission. Do a massive cleanout of what you're putting into your life and make sure whatever remains makes sense with your Innovated Identity. If it doesn't, purge!

Think About the *Where* in Your Life.

Our environment has a significant impact on us. Where do you often find yourself struggling with Comparison? Physical locations or scenarios? The gym? Awards ceremonies? Networking or social gatherings? A mom group surrounded by gossiping or judgmental moms? Perhaps even church? Some places may stimulate more tension than others. We can't (and shouldn't) avoid every situation where we notice ourselves comparing. Still, we do need to be very aware of these places, and in some cases, navigate a different direction for the time being.

When Comparison was driving my life, the thought of taking a vacation to the beach made me feel ill. I knew in advance the mental battles I'd be losing, while sitting among a beach full of other women who were more tanned, had nicer figures, and looked better in a bikini than I could ever hope to look. Sound familiar? Try choosing a different vacation destination for this time in your life—it's ok! Navigate your journey right now so you can continue to measure up to your Innovated Identity and win. The beach will still be there later.

A woman shared how she felt like such a bad mom whenever she went to her playgroup because her child was very spirited and not calm like the other children. Being around moms who could ask their children to use their inside voice with a positive result and get their kids to eat healthy food when her son wouldn't touch anything except chicken nuggets and vanilla wafers made her feel like she was doing something wrong. Attending the group sent her on a losing spiral with Comparison each week. No one wronged her, but it was time to find another community to join. And that's ok!

Listen, friend; you do not have to do this detrimental dance with Comparison in the elective areas of your life.

Don't allow people-pleasing, a membership to a gym, or coupons to stores that you know you shouldn't frequent, to be a roadblock to your Innovated Identity. It's not worth it! Avoid the major traps that get in the way. There are various places you can choose to frequent for now while you're growing in strength to claim control over Comparison.

Think About the *When* in Your Life.

As women, we know there are certain times that we are more susceptible to losing control to Comparison than others. Times of the day, times of the month, times of our life. Regardless of whether we are young, middle-aged, or elderly, hormones are often an unwelcome force that sways us one direction or the other. We have to face that truth. It can be difficult to watch a sappy life insurance commercial and have control over our tear ducts, so how in the world are we supposed to claim control over a force in our life like Comparison? Especially when our brains are swirling with irrational thoughts, and our bodies are under extra physical, emotional and chemical stress. Not to mention the realities of stuff like acne, bloating, menopause, weight gain, sexual changes, and other symptoms where Comparison sneaks up on us. There's not much we can do to change some of these circumstances. However, by being aware of the times that exacerbate our battles, we may be able to recognize sooner how to handle that icky feeling when Comparison begins to take the wheel, so we can navigate away.

If it's that time of the month, maybe it's not the best time to shop for bathing suits where the skinny swimsuit models on the signage are making you feel like a bloated, beached whale.

If you're extra sensitive to Comparison after a couple of glasses of wine, you may want to avoid late-night social gatherings that include drinking—or avoid alcohol when you're there. On that note, alcohol is proven to lower any filters we have set in place, and it reduces control in general, so being selective about where to allow yourself to indulge may help you better navigate your journey.

If late at night while lying in bed is when you wrestle with Comparison, perhaps you can identify new habits or bedtime routines to help guide your mindset before attempting your shut-eye.

If Comparison tends to take over when you're feeling like an outcast while eating in the break room at work, perhaps you can invite a friend to meet elsewhere for lunch. Or make a new friend at work who shares your interests and meet for lunch regularly.

The Gratitude Mindset.

It's difficult for Comparison to take control of our minds when we focus on the things for which we're thankful for. As simplistic as it sounds, it's true! Replacing some of our old thought patterns with new ones will help us to better navigate our journey. This takes practice since thankfulness doesn't come naturally but maintaining an attitude of gratitude will redirect your thinking nearly every time back toward your Innovated Identity. When doing chores, cleaning your home, and folding laundry, Comparison would have you fall into the mindset of: *Why can't my kids be helpful like other kids and help out with chores? If only I had money to hire a house cleaner like my friends! Gosh, my clothes are old and out of style!* Practicing an attitude of gratitude will instead spark thoughts along the lines of, *I'm so glad I was able to have children*, and *It's such a blessing to have a place to live*, and *I'm so grateful I've never been without clothing. Maybe I should go through and donate some items to the homeless shelter.*

Does this sound weird or impossible? It really isn't—but you must begin somewhere. Try starting with a gratitude journal. Keep it next to your bed. Before getting out of bed in the morning, write down three things you're grateful for, and before turning off the light at night, scribble down three more you were thankful for from your day. Catch yourself whenever you start to complain or compare and create an attitude of gratitude reversal. These reversals will become more innate and you'll become a pro before you know it!

Servanthood and Pressing In.

When it comes to swapping our Comparison mindset for an attitude of gratitude toward the people that we compare ourselves to, it can be a little trickier. It's hard to tell ourselves *I'm grateful for the woman sitting in the seat next to me on the plane traveling to Hawaii to speak at a huge conference, who flaunts pictures of her attractive husband and beautiful kids on her MacBook Pro while she's rocking the designer outfit I thought only existed in magazine ads.* Grrrr! How can I overcome the feeling of intimidation? This is when you need to make the definitive choice to kick Comparison to the curb for the moment and *press in.*

What would your Innovated Identity do? I guarantee she wouldn't snub and ignore. You may not feel like it but press into that person. Choose to get to know her and find ways to celebrate her accomplishments with her. See where you can connect and relate with one another.

Find ways to be of support or service to her. Servanthood trumps Comparison—it changes our mindset from self-focused to others-focused. When we look for ways to help someone, our mind switches into a different mode. We are more likely to see people for who they are instead of the better-than-me person we've made them out to be. We begin to trade out Comparison for Compassion.

Remember the woman I avoided at the conference, Dee? Our friendship is proof that *pressing in* works. I had to push Comparison out of my car and invite Dee to join me for a friendly drive. And Jenny, who pirated my post? I chose to *press in* and look at her differently, as well. By taking the chance to know her better instead of jumping to the most obvious conclusion—that she's a cutthroat content thief—I learned that she was naïve and needed some social media etiquette. We all need a little grace sometimes.

Self-Talk and Other Fuel.

Navigating our journey is more than avoiding the potholes. It's also about making sure we use the proper fuel to keep us going. The messages we put into our minds are powerful. Our brain absorbs more than we give it credit for, and we are in charge of what we expose it to. What we feed our soul is imperative to whether we claim control over Comparison or hand it the keys.

Are we speaking positive truth to ourselves or opting to spit negativity into our own faces? When we make a mistake, we can choose to call ourselves *stupid* or *idiot*, or we can make the choice to speak the truth and say *I made a mistake; I'll do better next time.* When we feel tired, we can tell ourselves and others how exhausted we are, or we can reframe and say *I could use some more rest.*

Make a concerted effort to identify negative self-talk and replace it with positive truth. Ask those around you to listen for this and to keep you accountable. These simple switches will make a difference in how you're able to stay in control over Comparison.

The music we listen to—is it uplifting? Does it convey positive messages that speak well about people, including ourselves, or does it cause us to think negatively, reminding us of relationships we *aren't* in, the fame we *don't* have, or how we don't measure up in some way?

Consider the consumption of news, movies, podcasts, and other messages our world of Comparison wants us to buy into often highlighting division and focusing on our inadequacies. Let's face it, there's so much coming at us and we need to be mindful of the agendas—intentional or not—that can creep into our psyche when we fail to live fully aware.

While avoiding the tangible roadblocks that get in our way is helpful, this alone will not give us the power we need to claim control over Comparison. The process of Navigating your Journey with behavioral modifications—such as refining your social media and canceling distracting subscriptions—are helpful, but they do not address the deeper issue. That is why many books and theories dealing with overcoming Comparison do not work—you can only get so far with behavioral changes. When you Navigate your Journey based on the premise of knowing what's at stake by weighing your cost in conjunction with innovating your identity to make the foundational changes, then you can change your beliefs and mindset. Behaviors will follow into alignment. One without the other is an incomplete approach.

Going back to our goal of eliminating the initial calculated expense list Comparison is costing us will be a telling sign whether or not we're making headway on your journey of controlling Comparison.

Hopefully this chapter sparked ideas for many behavioral modifications that will help you better align with your Innovated Identity and allow you to navigate a smoother journey. Act on some of those initial steps that came to mind and schedule a time for you to go through the who, what, where, and when arenas of your life. Then, maintain each one individually so you will have fewer collisions along the way!

On a scale of 1 to 10, how well are you currently Navigating Your Journey?

(pro navigator)   1 2 3 4 5 6 7 8 9 10   (help me!)

CHAPTER TEN

I'm winning! What's next?

> **Freedom** (n)
> The power or right to act, speak, or think as one wants without hindrance or restraint.

By this point, hopefully, you've begun to integrate the WIN Method to claim control over Comparison in your own life and are already experiencing and celebrating some wins! As women in this world, you and I have enormous daily challenges. Comparison constantly tempts us. Not only are we pitted against our wonderful female counterparts, but we're bombarded with messages reminding us to make sure we're not seen as lesser than our amazing male counterparts. The constant Comparison mentality can be exhausting.

The Male World of Comparison.

Though women have a heavy load when it comes to the world of Comparison, men are not immune to being hacked by Comparison. Though the takeover may look a little different, the root issue is still the same, and we need to be aware so we can be part of the solution.

In case you haven't figured out by now, I'm not a man. Therefore, I don't feel qualified to speak specifically for men merely through observations. However, I've observed a heck of a lot of Comparison-controlled living going on in the lives of men. To learn more, I've had intentional discussions with many men on this topic of Comparison. Most of them say at the beginning of the conversation that comparison isn't a huge issue in their lives. Still, as we talk and dive into the topic, it becomes apparent to us both that though we may not be using the same semantics, men are struggling with similar battles and are succumbing to the same costly outcomes. Comparison is hijacking them, too.

In a recent email I sent out to the people following this book's progress I asked, "In what ways has Comparison tried to navigate your journey?" One male subscriber bravely shared this response: "Comparison truly is the thief of joy. I've fallen into that trap so many times in my life. I'm not attractive. Real men don't have this problem. I'm not good enough."

While (most) men aren't busy eyeing one another's outfits or hair, plenty are comparing their vehicles and how much power they have, their businesses and capabilities, and even aspects of their significant other. They compare who can bench press the most, who makes the most money, who has the office with the best view, and who has the biggest guns (take that any way you want).

And let's not forget status and position—a common Comparison trap that our dear men fall prey to as well. What's the first thing that most gentlemen say to one another upon meeting for the first time?

"So, what do you do?"

While this is an innocent question asked to spark conversation and get to know the other person, it poses an instantaneous opportunity for Comparison to sneak in and take control. Either man in the situation can be affected.

Let's do a hypothetical role play.

Meet Gary and Cory. Both men are in their 50s, have never met, and are sitting in the auto dealership waiting for their car to be returned from an oil change. They eventually strike up a conversation, and Gary poses the classic question, "So, what do you do?"

Cory replies, "I'm an attorney. I've been practicing law over at ABC Law Firm on Main Street for about 25 years. How about you; what do you do?"

Gary had been out of work for a while, but recently began working as a teller at the local bank. There's a good chance he's going to feel a little lower in status compared to his new acquaintance.

However, if the same conversation occurred except Cory (the attorney) was to have said that he worked at McDonald's as a cashier, Gary would feel better about himself and his new position at the bank.

I was recently having lunch with several acquaintances: a banker, an attorney, and a small business owner. We saw each other in a business environment about once per month where we shared the occasional friendly small talk.

This particular day was a little different. While the conversation began with the typical greeting, "Hey, how's it going?" it quickly evolved into a deeper discussion when the attorney pointed at my open laptop and asked what I was working on.

I told him that I was writing a book. When he asked what it was about, I simply said, "Comparison." I figured the topic would be dead amongst this table of professional men, and the small talk about sports and weather would resume. However, the attorney surprised me and continued the conversation.

"Comparison, huh?" he replied animatedly. "I need that book when you're done with it. But not for myself—for everyone around me!"

He went on to share that his 20-something old son—who's a well-known, self-made social media star—struggles with Comparison. "He travels all over the world as well-known companies pay him more than you can imagine. He makes his own schedule, gets to do everything he loves to do, and he has over a million followers. He's got it all, but he sees his friends and other guys his age settling down with girlfriends and getting married. He compares himself with them and thinks, 'What's wrong with me? Why don't I have that?'"

We made some small talk about the millennial generation and how this social media stuff has taken its toll on Millennials (apparently, they didn't realize that I'm a Millennial). I looked over at the banker, Adam, who was quiet but listening intently. In a quick effort to keep the conversation alive, I asked, "So, Adam, what do you think is the primary area that business professionals struggle with, when it comes to the issue of Comparison?"

"Me?" he asked, eyes widely looking around, hoping I was talking to someone else.

I smiled and nodded.

Without hesitation, as if he had been processing the topic the whole time, he blurted out, "Promotions."

Comparison isn't merely a female problem as many may believe—it's a human problem. Despite the countless commercials for hair products, skin creams, and plastic surgery, Comparison affects both genders, all ages, and fellow human beings of every culture, race, and demographic.

Comparison wants to control, and will attempt to gain it through any angle it possibly can. It creeps into our media and tries to divide us by making our differences seem like some great chasm that can never be crossed. Our uniqueness seems better or worse through social movements and dividing topics focused around race, gender, demographics, and political affiliations. While these discussions need to be had to make a difference in our world, before we run and stake our lives on a cause or identify with one side or another, let's stop and think about the effect that taking a side could have not only on our own lives, but our culture as a whole. Let's step back and take a bigger picture approach to recognize one commonality that we can all relate to— one common ground that we can all stand on:

We are all human.

American Idol alumni and music artist Mandisa has a hit song entitled *Bleed the Same* with lyrics that help to put our shared humanity into perspective: "Pointing fingers, taking sides . . . We all bleed the same." Yes, underneath all of our stuff, we are all imperfect human beings battling Comparison in some way.

It's sad to watch as Comparison's control seems to intensify with each generation—navigating quicker into the human psyche via technology, social definitions of success, and the growing statistics and acceptance of self-focused and narcissistic thinking.

We must not expect change to happen on its own; we need to be the catalyst in our private spheres of influence and in our communities. We are the role models, the teachers, the couriers who will pass along the knowledge and message that measuring up isn't defined by asset acquisition, appearances or achievements. It's up to us to sing the freedom anthem that winning in this world doesn't mean you have to be what everyone else says you should be.

Viewing Comparison as a global problem can make it seem overwhelming—perhaps hopeless—to imagine substantial or lasting change. After all, you can only control your response and your actions, right?

Yes, you can only do *you*. However, how you choose to do you can create ripples of change. Think of the many seemingly hopeless endeavors once thought as impossible, such as women's suffrage or the civil rights movement. It takes individuals, person by person, standing up for what's right to erect change in thinking. You must believe that freedom from Comparison is a possibility.

Your Words.

Words are powerful. Too often, we carelessly spit them out and toss them around, ignorant of the fact that they're being interpreted and digested differently by everyone around us. While Comparison can be beneficial, we know it can also take people down a dead-end street—and your words can be the fuel propelling them in that direction.

There are obvious phrases used intentionally to make a person feel intimidated by Comparison. An example would be blatantly saying that they don't measure up or that they're not as good as another person. Hopefully those instances are few and far between. However, what if I told you that your everyday speech could unintentionally be causing others to struggle with Comparison without you realizing it?

Let's not get too academic or cause bad elementary school flashbacks, but think back to Language Arts class where you learned about the comparative and superlative for adjectives and adverbs. Basically, we put a suffix after adjectives and adverbs to make them describe in terms of degrees: comparative is the second or middle degree, and superlative is the third or highest degree.[33]

Let's use Nina, a middle school student, for a practical example. Look at the series of sentences below and notice how putting -er or -est after the adjective *hard*, could be potentially harmful to hear if you were one of Nina's classmates. See if you notice why:

Nina works harder than she did last year in school.
Nina works hardest when she's by herself.
Nina works harder than others in school.
Nina works the hardest in her class.

Can you tell the difference between the first two and the second two? The first two statements compare Nina against herself. The latter two sentences compare Nina against her classmates. If you're one of Nina's classmates, you may feel compared to Nina's work ethic, even though you and your work ethic weren't explicitly thought of when I wrote those sentences. Nonetheless, it doesn't stop your mind from going to the land of Comparison and wondering, *Do I measure up? Am I good enough? What makes Nina so special?* We need to be aware of our words and how they sound to others.

Some of the common comparative words we use are:

- Best, Better
- More, Most
- Less, Least
- Worse, Worst

I see this often with young ladies who frequently post pictures of themselves together with friends on social media. It puzzles me when they'll share a picture with a girlfriend and a caption that reads *Best friends forever!* one day and the next, they tag a different friend with *#bestfriends* and hours later, a selfie image captioned *I'm so glad we're best friends!* pops up.

How can each friend be the *best*? Maybe *one of the best,* but there's only one *best.* When we use superlative terms about people, there's always a risk of others reading into the situation and feeling the seatbelt of Comparison tightening. We don't know what people are going through on the other side of a screen. I've witnessed women who've felt they were mutually close with a particular friend, but after seeing their friend post endearing words about other friends and never about her, she questioned the depth of their friendship. Did she not measure up? Maybe they weren't great friends, after all? I'm not here to tell anyone how to talk or that it's wrong to have many so-called best friends, but I am here to ask you to consider your word choices and, perhaps, consider paring down the superlative statements to be used only when they're undoubtedly true. It will make your words more genuine, and as an added benefit they will carry more weight.

Whether intentional or not, when others believe we don't see them as measuring up in some way, it can play a part in racking up negative costs in their life. Keep in mind that a seemingly innocent comment made by Prince Charles affected Princess Diana to the point of triggering a psychological response resulting in some painful consequences.

Friends, you're not traveling alone on this highway of life. To change this world that is dominated by Comparison, we need to have the mindset of being the

Good Samaritan and help others learn to measure up the right way. Awareness of the potential power behind our language is an essential part of being a good role model. It's contagious in both directions; controlling Comparison in your life should encourage you to help other people move toward experiencing that same freedom. While you can't (and shouldn't try to) drive someone else's journey for them, you can be a sign or a billboard pointing them in the right direction. Every life that's been positively impacted has the potential to create more culture-changing billboards along the way.

Celebrate Differences.

My friend Nellie and I sat on the bleachers talking at a track meet. I thoroughly enjoy her company as we have so much in common: faith, same-aged children, positive outlooks. Somehow the topic of skin color entered our conversation. Nellie has dark skin and was born in Kenya—I have very light skin and have lived in the state of Ohio in the United States for my entire life. We chatted about the beautiful differences in pigment and how blessed we were to see so many cultures and backgrounds represented in our community. Our society shouldn't be colorblind; we should celebrate the many colors of humanity!

Instead of it being normalized to bring up diverse conversations in order to learn about others, most people avoid it in fear of offending people who are different than themselves. She shared with me her experience of being a teacher with dark skin and how she wanted to help the younger generation recognize that many phrases and thoughts come across as offensive due to the way history and literature portrays groups of people. It's learned ignorance.

Nellie pointed out that people in America are more sensitive to racial discussions than other areas of the world, primarily due to defensiveness about the past and the uncertainty of how to approach and interact with people in the present. I asked her opinion on how we could bridge this gap of not wanting to offend, nor wanting to be hurt. She said we should have more open conversations. We need to *choose* not to be offended or defensive and also give others the benefit of the doubt when they may seem to be coming across wrong. We can kindly correct people and shed light on intentional and unintentional offenses in a positive and non-shaming way when we hear them being spoken. Many people from older generations grew up using derogatory terms that were acceptable at the time, but we now know are offensive to people of color. Yet, they still use them, and we can't expect people to learn if they're not made aware. Many people from our parents' and grandparents' generations read these now offensive ways of speech in history books—or even lived and experienced the pain, prejudice, and tension firsthand. We don't know what anyone has gone through and what has caused them to say what they say or think the way they think. Let's be intentional to see people as individuals, and not group them according to race, ethnic background, age, etc. When we stereotype, Comparison has already won. People do not choose when or where they were born, what family, financial status, intelligence, or skin they were born into—but they do choose their thoughts and actions as they move forward in life.

I have a passion for cultures and diversity. There's something Heavenly about all of the differences, colors, traditions, ways of doing things, and, of course, food! It's fun to celebrate how similar and yet how different we all are. When I was in my late teens, I began attending a multicultural church that consisted of people from all over the world. As a white American, I was the minority—and I loved it. Growing up, I lived in a city where there were only *black*, *white*, and *biracial* people, so this newfound diversity was a refreshing experience. One day in church, when describing one friend to another, I used the word *oriental* as a description. I had no idea it was an offensive term, as it had no derogatory connotations for me. It's the term I had heard growing up, and no one intended it negatively.

Thankfully, a friend pulled me aside and kindly corrected me. "Renee, when you call someone 'oriental,' you're basically calling them a rug. The correct term is Asian." I felt so bad for my mistake, knowing that I had unintentionally called people rugs over my short lifetime, and yet, I was so grateful for this friend pulling me aside to teach me kindly. She made a cultural difference that day. I've since been able to do the same for many people who've also grown up with outdated and ignorant terms.

Let's open up these conversations, being kind and non-shaming when we correct. Give people the benefit of the doubt and be quick to accept and slow to judge. We each have so much to learn—why not learn from one another? In doing so, we can decrease Comparison's grip on our world as we continue to win.

My Impact.

For the past several years, I've been working through this topic—contemplating, learning, experimenting, and growing in this area of claiming control over Comparison in my life. Sharing my thoughts along the way, I encounter apathy and hopelessness at times, but most people do see the effects of Comparison and long to experience change. A common theme while talking with women is a yearning for community with other women who also want to claim control over Comparison. We want a safe place where we can let our guards down and each be seen as the worthy, significant ladies we are. We want to feel like we measure up and can connect with others—and want them to accept our good-hearted intentions. We crave a place that discourages pretenses while encouraging authenticity and vulnerability—a place where we can leave our masks at the door and be accepted for simply being the person we were created to be.

This message of *Measuring Up* is where I am staking my billboard and attempting to make a difference for others. The book in your hand is only the beginning. Being a connector is one aspect of my Innovated Identity. I love to connect with people, encourage them, help them to see their potential, and freely be authentic. It's rewarding to do that one-on-one for individuals and also in a small group atmosphere through coaching, but what if I could make a difference on a larger scale? What if I could create a space specifically where women can leave their masks behind; where titles are irrelevant, all skin colors and backgrounds are celebrated, and women are loved for who they are—not for what they look like, what they have, or what they've achieved?

This is my passion, and I get excited just typing this! Imagine, if I—a girl who once was so focused on comparing myself to others—could create a community that put Comparison in its place and make a substantial impact teaching and training women how to control Comparison in their own lives. Even more, what if those women modeled the same in their influential realms? Their daughters learned from an early age to claim control over Comparison. Other women felt the difference and felt free and unthreatened in their presence, so they began to ask questions and learn the reason for the counter-cultural mindset?

Well, it's happening! I launched the group and people are coming together, setting aside their intimidation, and changing their mindset. They're bringing their weaknesses and shortcomings forward allowing others to help them with their strengths, and vice versa. We are all a work in process and we can grow when we're permitted to be authentic. If a group like this interests you, learn more at www.reneevidor.com.

Your Impact.

Take a peek at your Innovated Identity. As you continue to measure up to it and win, what are some ways you can help share this message? When you begin living out who you're created to be, what you're designed to do will become more evident. Not only can you save time, money, energy, and live free by measuring up and winning in this world of Comparison, but you can use talents and passions unique to you to cultivate the same freedom for those who are in your sphere of influence—children, coworkers, friends, family, prospects, clients, strangers you meet in the grocery store. Measuring up can be contagious and has the potential to impact others.

Cutting back on the Comparison costs will allow you to begin viewing the world differently. As you become empowered by this new outlook, you'll start to empower others. Continue working out your identity process, and as you learn to become who you were created to be, those around you will feel the freedom to become their authentic selves too. Trade your fake ID for your Innovated Identity and your newfound confidence will give license to onlookers to look into the horizon for their destination and begin navigating their journey instead of the detour that the world of Comparison wants for them. It's a ripple effect that never stops.

A Final Thought.

Remember how I said this is a life-long journey and that it only gets better as you navigate it to win? I'm excited to leave you with one final example.

This manuscript for *Measuring Up* was complete, and I was working through the first round of edits when my life got interrupted. Though it marks an exceedingly challenging time, the interruption actually brought this book full-circle. I knew the WIN Method worked, but now I had physical proof—a real-life experience that passed the test beyond the head and heart knowledge.

Previously I shared with you that I had undergone a breast augmentation. This was back in 2010 (nine years before completing the manuscript for Measuring Up). Occasionally I felt a twinge of phoniness for having implants; however, rarely did I give them a second thought. Until July 4, 2019.

Despite being in my mid-thirties and having an active healthy lifestyle, strange health concerns began to surface early in 2019. My health quickly declined. Symptoms such as sudden-onset of asthma, heart palpitations, numbness, brain fog, anxiety, vision issues, unexplainable fatigue, pain, and many other abnormalities kept me from my normal activities including public speaking, social gatherings, and even grocery shopping. Doctors observed my symptoms yet wrote me off as healthy, attributing my issues to getting older. In my gut, I knew something was wrong. Very wrong.

The evening of July 4th, 2019, after a usual bout of migraine and fatigue, I told my sweet mama who was visiting that I "couldn't go on like this," to which she replied, "Renee, please, research your breast implants." She knew someone who had recently had them removed and regained her health. I promised I would do some research, but inside I was thinking, *How could my nine-year-old fake boobs have anything to do with all of these weird symptoms?*

Later that night, I was pushing through the brain fog attempting to work on the cover design for *Measuring Up* when I saw it: a book cover with the title, *Are Your Fake Boobs Making You Sick?* by author Jen Hererra.[34] I immediately dropped my work, and began to research the author. My foggy world began to see a ray of clarity due to a non-coincidental introduction to something called *Breast Implant Illness* (*BII*). Jen shared her experience with this BII and the list of her symptoms matched what I was experiencing—*and* how they greatly improved or went away once she removed her implants.

I felt shaken to the core. Had I found the answer to my mysterious debilitating illness? If so, how would I deal with having my implants removed? A roller coaster of emotions and questions flooded my brain, but deep down, I knew what I needed to do (and needed to do quickly).

The next day, while I continued to research, learn, and process BII, a dear friend's Facebook post revealed that she, too, was dealing with all of these symptoms and was scheduled to have her implants removed later that month. That made the third sign within a few days on a topic about which I previously knew nothing. I joined a Facebook group that had, at that time, over 80,000 female members sharing their all-too-familiar stories. Many of those women had undergone the removal of their implants (also known as an "explant" procedure) and reported amazing improvements.

Without delay, I made the necessary calls and appointments. So much internal processing went on in my brain. How would I feel going back to the original physical state that I paid a lot of money to alter? Would I look terrible? Would measuring up to my Innovated Identity get me through this, or would Comparison take control of my appearances once again, as I let it nine years prior? What if I didn't get well?

It was during this time of weighing my cost that I also made the conscious decision to *Navigate my Journey* in advance. I chose to be me—authentically and unapologetically—to love me, and to live *me*. In short, I *would* measure up to my Innovated Identity! I didn't wait to find out; I made up my mind of what the outcome would be. Looking back, this was integral to my success.

I went all in, sharing on social media what I had been going through, the impending surgery, and then updates afterward. I'm happy to report that after removing my implants on September 9, 2019, my health showed immediate improvement—by the following day! When my mom visited me post-surgery, she was thrilled that I was able to play two games of Scrabble® in a row (our favorite pastime), whereas I hadn't been able to finish a single game without falling asleep for the past couple of years. The brain fog cleared, the numbness left, my breathing and vision improved, and I was speaking again to large groups within three weeks post-explant! In six weeks, I was confidently speaking on a stage to several hundred businesspeople about this message of *Measuring Up*—now with an even greater story and as a walking visual billboard.

It's funny how life works sometimes. It seemed that I had removed all of my masks, but two of them were sewn inside of me needing to come out so that I could physically confirm that, yes, by the grace of God, the process outlined in this book really works. Here's how the WIN Method helped me in my journey from choosing to get implants to my explant procedure:

My decision to have a breast augmentation arose due to my insecurity and belief that others *looked* better than I did. When I discovered my implants were causing my health issues, I performed a Cost Analysis of what Comparison had already, and would continue to cost me. The Cost Analysis revealed that my Comparison-driven implants were very expensive: initially they cost me money and downtime from surgery and were currently costing me my physical health, mental health, and overall productivity. Additionally, they were costing my family the daughter, wife, mother and friend they deserved. Next, I looked at who I was *currently* and who I *wanted* to be moving forward—then I measured myself against my Innovated Identity. It didn't take long for me to make a solid mental shift toward the fact that, for me, winning meant that my appearance wasn't a crucial aspect of my Innovated Identity and I therefore had nothing to worry about.

Post surgery, not only has Comparison not been a struggle for me in that area, but I've realized I'm grateful and satisfied with who I was created to be and how I was created to look. My body *shame* has been swapped out for body *gratitude*. After all, measuring up has nothing to do with size (including bra size).

Our journey with Comparison and measuring up properly will continue on with different seasons and destinations until the day we reach our final destination. We must constantly weigh our cost, innovate our identity, and navigate our journey to win in this world of Comparison.

It's up to you. Will you stay enslaved and keep trying to measure up to the crazy antics of Comparison-controlled thinking? Or, will you choose the freedom that comes through measuring up when you follow the roadmap to WIN? If you want to win in the world of Comparison, you have to chose not to lose . . . choose not to lose control, that is.

I trust you'll make the right choice.

Look for me, waving with a friendly smile as I cheer you on from the next lane over, sister!

On a scale of 1 to 10, how well do you know your destination? If you could use some help in this area, remember to check out ComparisonBook.com/resources for roadside assistance on your journey!

(very well)   1 2 3 4 5 6 7 8 9 10   (no clue)

ACKNOWLEDGMENTS

My amazing family—Josh, Nathan, Ariela, Dad, Mom, Mike, Becca—you'll never know what your patience and support throughout this long project mean to me. I love each of you.

To my many friends (you know who you are), including Wendy, my editor Gailyc, and Mark and Shelly Photography (photo credit next page), thank you for your moral and physical support of this project.

Thanks to the pilot group members that helped to get this plane off the ground: Joann Balliett, Beth Dalvi, Becky Davis, Jeff Elder, Haydi Labib, and Bill Morrow.

Chick-Fil-A Sawmill Road staff, I appreciate all of you who became like family as I wrote *Measuring Up* in my corner booth #17 in your store.

Above all, thank you God for entrusting this message of *Measuring Up* with me to share with others.

ABOUT THE AUTHOR

 As authentic as they come, Renee Vidor is an author, speaker, and community creator who helps individuals and organizations discover how to be who they're created to be so that they can do what they're designed to do. Renee and her husband, Josh, live in Ohio with their two wonderful teenagers. When she's not spending time with her family or running a business, Renee enjoys walks with friends, traveling, nature, and dark chocolate. Lots of dark chocolate. Connect with her at ReneeVidor.com

YOUR NEXT STEPS
WITH *MEASURING UP*

 EXPERIENCE THE FREE ASSESSMENT
DETERMINE YOUR COMPARAHOLIC SCORE

 TAKE THE 6-WEEK COURSE
DEVELOP YOUR ROADMAP TO WIN

 JOIN THE MISSION
BECOME A CERTIFIED COACH - SPEAKER - TRAINER

COMPARISONBOOK.COM

RENEE VIDOR

A DYNAMIC SPEAKER FOR YOUR:

- CONFERENCE
- RETREAT
- WORKSHOP
- TEAM BUILDING EVENT

WHEN YOU BRING RENEE INTO YOUR BUSINESS OR NON-PROFIT YOU
WILL GET AN AUTHENTIC, INSPIRING, AND CUSTOMIZED EXPERIENCE.

LEARN MORE AT RENEEVIDOR.COM

ENDNOTES

1   Mary. (2018, March 11). Leon Festinger's Social Comparison Theory. Retrieved November 10, 2019, from https://www.psychologynoteshq.com/leonfestinger-socialcomparisontheory/.

2   Ibid.

3   Ibid.;

4   Rhodes, Marjorie, and Brickman, Daniel. "New Study Explores Social Comparison in Early Childhood." Association for Psychological Science—APS. Psychological Science, a journal of the Association for Psychological Science, October 2008. https://www.psychologicalscience.org/news/releases/new-study-explores-social-comparison-in-early-childhood.html

5   Patten, Eileen. "Racial, Gender Wage Gaps Persist in U.S. Despite Some Progress." Pew Research Center, July 1, 2016. https://www.pewresearch.org/fact-tank/2016/07/01/racial-gender-wage-gaps-persist-in-u-s-despite-some-progress/.

6   https://www.today.com/style/woman-defends-tiny-wedding-ring-powerful-facebook-post-t85501

7   Keeping up with the Joneses: Inequality and Indebtedness, in the Era of the Housing Price Bubble, 1999-2007* Neil Fligstein, Pat Hastings, and Adam Goldstein Department of Sociology University of California Berkeley, Ca. 94610 August 2015. https://wwwophastings.com/publication/fligsteinhastingsgoldstein2017/.

8   History's Women. Accessed November 1, 2019. https://www.historyswomen.com/history-in-the-making/joni-eareckson-tada/.

9   Katz, Neil. "Life-Size Barbie's Shocking Dimensions (PHOTO): Would She Be Anorexic?" CBS News. CBS Interactive, April 21, 2011. https://www.cbsnews.com/news/life-size-barbies-shocking-dimensions-photo-would-she-be-anorexic/

10   Perrin, Andrew. "Social Media Usage: 2005-2015." Pew Research Center: Internet, Science & Tech, October 12, 2015. http://www.pewinternet.org/2015/10/08/social-networking-usage-2005-2015/

11   Smith, Kurt, Lmft, and Lpcc. "Why Men Watch Porn—8 Things Women Need to Know About Internet Porn." Counseling for Men, September 27, 2017. https://www.guystuffcounseling.com/counseling-men-blog/bid/24369/why-men-watch-porn-8-things-women-need-to-know-about-internet-porn

12   Gregory, Christina. "Narcissistic Personality Disorder (NPD): Causes, Symptoms, Treatment." Psycom.net—Mental Health Treatment Resource Since 1986, October 22, 2019. https://www.psycom.net/personality-disorders/narcissistic/.

13   "Global Cosmetics Products Market Expected to Reach USD 805.61 Billion by 2023." Reuters. Thomson Reuters, March 13, 2018.
https://www.reuters.com/brandfeatures/venture-capital/article?id=30351.
14   Haynes, Chelsea. "True Cost of Beauty: Survey Reveals Where American Spend Most." GrouponMerchant, August 7, 2019.
https://www.groupon.commerchant/blog/true-cost-beauty-americans-spend-most-survey.
15   Ibid.
16   The Annual Bullying Survey 2017: What 10,000 People Told Us About Bullying." Ditch the Label, July 2017.
https://www.ditchthelabel.org/research-papers/the-annual-bullying-survey-2017/.
17   Karnick, Ruby. "50 Facts About Meryl Streep—Margaret Thatcher, from 'The Iron Lady.'" BOOMSbeat, December 29, 2015.
https://www.boomsbeat.com/articles/105886/20151229/50-facts-meryl-streep-margaret-thatcher-iron-lady.htm
18   "Meryl Streep." IMDb. IMDb.com. Accessed November 18, 2019.
https://www.imdb.com/name/nm0000658/awards.
19   Schrotenboer, Brent. "How the Oprah Confession Has Weighed on Lance Armstrong." USA Today. Gannett Satellite Information Network, January 23, 2018.
https://www.usatoday.com/story/sports/2018/01/16/how-oprah-confession-has-weighed-lance-armstrong/1035056001/.
20   Dee, Angela. *Voiceless: Spencer's Story—A Mother's Journey Raising a Son with Significant Needs. Powell, OH: Author Academy Elite, 2016.*

21 "The Panorama Interview with the Princess of Wales." BBC News. BBC, November 20, 1995.

22 Morton, Andrew. *Diana: Her True Story—In Her Own Words*. London: Michael OMara Books Limited, 2019.

23 Mowbray, Nicole. "Oprah's Path to Power." The Guardian. Guardian News and Media, March 2, 2003. https://www.theguardian.com/media/2003/mar/02/pressandpublishing.usnews1.

24 Swarns, Rachel L. "The Science Behind 'They All Look Alike to Me'." *The New York Times*, September 20, 2015. https://www.nytimes.com/2015/09/20/nyregion/the-science-behind-they-all-look-alike-to-me.html

25 Layton, Lyndsey. "Once Bullied, Now Empowered, Lizzie Velasquez Lobbies Capitol Hill." The Washington Post. WP Company, October 27, 2015.

26 https://en.wikipedia.org/wiki/Lizzie_Vel%C3%A1squez

27 Oliver, Amy. "World's 'Ugliest Woman' Lizzie Velasquez Gives Courageous Interview." *Daily Mail Online*. Associated Newspapers, September 13, 2012. https://www.dailymail.co.uk/news/article-2202512/Worlds-ugliest-woman-Lizzie-Velasquez-gives-courageous-interview.html#axzz2KCWRMnw7.

28 Layton, Lyndsey. "Once Bullied, Now Empowered, Lizzie Velasquez Lobbies Capitol Hill." *The Washington Post*. WP Company, October 27, 2015. https://www.washingtonpost.com/local/education/once-bullied-now-empowered-lizzie-velasquez-lobbies-capitol-hill/2015/10/27/8f6c8ece-7ce3-11e5-afce-2afd13eb896_story.html?noredirect=on.

29 Velasquez, Lizzie. "How Do YOU Define Yourself?" TEDxAustinWomen. December 2013.

https://www.ted.com/talks/lizzie_velasquez_how_do_you_define_yourself?language=en.

30 https://en.wikipedia.org/wiki/Lizzie_Vel%C3%A1squez

31 https://www.google.com/search?q=Dictionary#dobs=navigate

32 "To Cut Down a Tree in Five Minutes Spend Three Minutes Sharpening Your Axe." Quote Investigator, January 14, 2019. https://www.quoteinvestigator.com/2014/03/29/sharp-axe/.

33 ATLAS, University of Illinois, and Urbana-Champaign. "Writers Workshop: Writer Resources Grammar Handbook." The Center for Writing Studies, Illinois, 2013. https://www.cws.illinois.edu/workshop/writers/comparatives/.

34 Herrera, Jen. Are Your Fake Boobs Making You Sick? JenHerreraTV, 2018.

CPSIA information can be obtained
at www.ICGtesting.com
Printed in the USA
LVHW021522050720
659666LV00005B/316